Mel Bay's

# Beginning Country Guitar Handbook

### By Dix Bruce

- Bass Runs
- How to Play Leads
- Eighteen Great Songs
- Basic Backup Technique
- Introductory Music Theory
- Transposing from One Key to Another
- "Sources" Section for Further Study
- Complete Play-Along Cassette Tape
- Hammer-Ons, Pull-Offs, and Slides
- Seven Fiddle Tunes for Guitar
- Soloing and Improvisation

**A stereo cassette tape of the music in this book is now available. The publisher strongly recommends the use of this cassette tape along with the text to insure accuracy of interpretation and ease in learning.**

Dedicated with love to my mother, Genevieve, and Al and Phyllis Weiner.

Special thanks for editorial assistance from John Blasquez, Kathi Bruce, Brian Pardo, and Duane Wong.

# Contents

---

**Dix Bruce** is a musician, writer and award-winning guitar player from the San Francisco Bay Area. He edited **Mandolin World News** from 1978 to 1984 and has recorded two albums with bluegrass legend Frank Wakefield. He recently completed a solo folk recording, *My Folk Heart,* and has just released a band recording of string swing & jazz, *Tuxedo Blues,* with many of his original compositions.

# Introduction

The flatpicked guitar has always been an important and defining presence in bluegrass and country music. As both a rhythm and a lead instrument it has shaped the sounds of artists from The Carter Family and Jimmy Rogers in the early days to Dwight Yoacum, Ricky Skaggs, and Hot Rise today. The basic flatpicking technique is simple and incredibly versatile. Students can develop it to the highest levels of lead improvisation. Whether you play in your home for your own enjoyment or expect someday to play the big stages with the big acts, you'll find flatpicking a rewarding technique and great fun.

**This book will:**

• **Explain the basics of guitar flatpicking.**

• **Offer exercises to improve your rhythm and lead playing.**

• **Present a repertoire of tunes to help you perfect your flatpicking technique and increase your overall knowledge of the guitar.**

All the music and tablature printed in this book can be heard on the accompanying stereo, split-track cassette.

★　　　★　　　★　　　★　　　★　　　★　　　★　　　★

Before we begin, let's answer the question *"What is flatpicking?"* Quite simply put, **flatpicking** is an approach to guitar playing that uses (guess what?) a flatpick! The player holds the flatpick between the thumb and first finger of the picking hand and strums chords and/or picks out melodies.

This technique differs from classical and folk "fingerpicking" where the bare fingers or "fingerpicks" (special curved thumb and finger picks) are used to play the strings.

Generically the term "flatpicking" applies to the way that most pop, rock, country, jazz, blues, and bluegrass guitarists play. Virtually every technique outlined in this book can be useful in any of these styles. Specifically, though, the term "flatpicking" is used to define a certain type of music more in the folk-bluegrass and country realm. In its simplest form flatpicking is a style of rhythm and lead playing that incorporates a picked bass note followed by a chord strum. (See Example 1.) More advanced playing is typified by rapid-fire eighth- or sixteenth-note melodies played without strums. (See Example 2 or Tunes 24–31.)

# Example 1

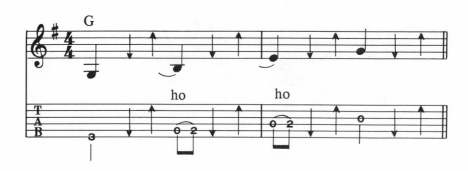

# Example 2

Most of the material in this book is based on the playing of traditional American country guitarists like Mother Maybelle Carter of the Carter Family, Doc Watson, Clarence White, Tony Rice, Dan Crary, Norman Blake, and others. Nearly all of these players use or used acoustic, unamplified, flat-top, steel-string guitars, usually Martins or Gibsons, to achieve their characteristic country sound. If you don't have an acoustic flat-top, don't worry. These tunes and techniques, while sounding slightly different, will work perfectly well on any guitar, acoustic or electric, nylon or steel-string.

I cannot stress enough the value of learning by listening to the music of flatpickers. See it live, watch what the players do, and study recordings thoroughly. It's the only way to understand what's basically an aural folk art form. The discography in the back of this book will help you get started.

★　　★　　★　　★　　★　　★　　★　　★

Learning to flatpick is definitely a hands-on pursuit. It's especially important to *play* this music every chance you get with friends, at jam sessions, or along with records. It's the only way to train your fingers and your musical sensibility.

The accompanying cassette tape is helpful for both listening and playing practice. Play along with it as you study the exercises and tunes in the book. Everything is presented in stereo, most things at both slow and regular speeds, with rhythm and lead separated left and right so that by adjusting the balance control of your stereo you can listen to and play along with either or both.

To simplify using the cassette tape, zero your counter at the very beginning of each side. Then write the counter numbers beside each exercise in the book (e.g., "exercise 5-A 206" or "exercise 32-B 105" — letters denote tape sides) as you go through the tape the first time. Individual sections of the tape will then be a snap to find. (We didn't include counter numbers in the tape package because the counters of individual cassette machines vary so greatly.)

To begin the exercises and tunes, you'll need a rudimentary knowledge of the guitar and guitar chords. The chords you'll need to know are in Chart 3 on page 10. The numbers on the grid represent fretting-finger numbers: 1 = index, 2 = middle, 3 = ring, 4 = pinkie, T = thumb. "X" above the grid means that string should not be sounded. You should either not pick it or dampen it with your fretting hand. The numbers below the grid denote which part of the chord each string supplies. I'll explain this in more detail later. Right now just make sure that you can play and easily change all of the chords shown by trying a few of the songs in this book. Practice those chords that are unfamiliar or give you difficulty. Skip the ones that you know.

If you're not used to holding a flatpick, be patient. No doubt it'll fly out of your hand now and then at the least opportune time. Your hand may also cramp up until you find just the right amount of pressure to hold it securely. Again, patience. Your pick grip is crucial to everything you play. Since I can't be there with you physically, it might be worth your while to enlist some in-person teacher advice to get you started on the right foot, or in this case, the right hand! An experienced teacher can also help you choose a guitar that's relatively easy to play. The action should be relatively low, but without string buzzes.

I use a Fender heavy teardrop-shaped pick. I recommend that you try several different brands of medium and heavy picks and that you stay away from thins, at least for now. I hold the pick between the thumb and index finger of my right hand. The photo below shows how I hold the pick.

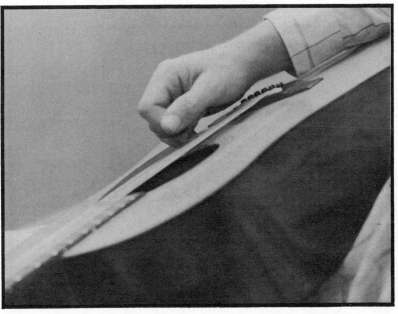

Photo by Al Weiner

When I strum, the fourth finger of my right hand brushes the pickguard on the guitar. When I pick continuous melody notes I loosely anchor my fourth finger on the pickguard. There's a great deal of controversy over whether a player should anchor a finger or develop a free-swinging picking hand which "pivots" from the wrist or elbow. A non-anchored hand probably offers the capability of developing great speed. An anchored hand may provide a stronger picking stroke. Over time you'll develop your own approach, but for now try both and concentrate on finding a comfortable position. If it hurts, you're doing something wrong. Hold the pick firmly, but without tension. More on this later.

I tend to pick the strings over the soundhole nearer the bridge than the end of the fingerboard. That's where most things sound the best on *my* guitar. Yours may be different. I change this hand position to slightly alter the sound; moving toward the fingerboard gives me a mellow sound, toward the bridge a punchier, more trebly sound.

Use a guitar strap whenever you play, either in the sitting or standing position. Sometimes it's difficult for students to make the transition from sitting to standing. Use of a strap from the beginning can ease this transition.

Photo by Al Weiner

Those of you who don't read standard music notation will find tablature directly under the standard notation. Since tablature styles differ, here's a short primer on the tab used in this book. If you read standard notation, you may find the tablature helpful in determining fret positions.

The six lines (see next page) represent the six strings of the guitar. The bottom line represents the sixth or lowest-sounding string; the top string represents the first or highest-sounding string. The others follow in between. Numbers represent the fret numbers on the guitar neck where the notes are played. Circled numbers above the tab staff (not on lines) represent fretting-hand fingers, just like the chord diagrams in Chart 3: 1 = index, 2 = middle, 3 = ring, 4 = pinkie, T = thumb.

Rhythm is shown similar to that of standard notation. In tablature, circled numbers on lines represent half ② and whole ④ notes.

Quarter notes look like this ¹| ; eighths like this ¹♭ . These tab symbols have the same time value as the standard notes on which they're based. In 4/4 and 3/4, a whole note = four counts, a half note = 2 counts, a quarter note = 1 count, an eighth note = ½ count (or two eighth notes = 1 count). Hammers (ho), pulls (po), and slides (sl) are represented by the abbreviations shown or slur markings, ⌣ or ⌐ , and string bends are shown enclosed by parentheses ⁽⁶⁾ .

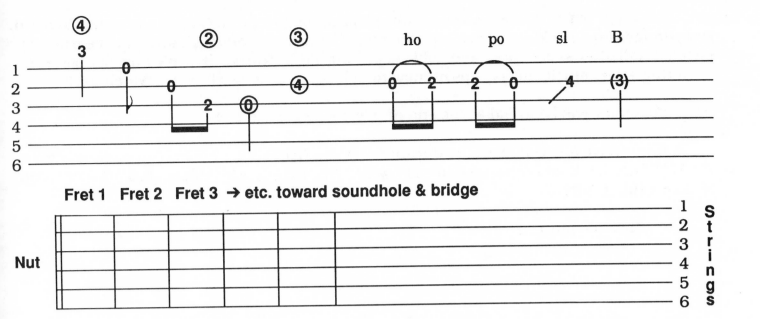

**Fret 1   Fret 2   Fret 3 → etc. toward soundhole & bridge**

Throughout this book, I offer extra study suggestions with almost every tune. It's important that you work through them on your own. You'll easily double or triple your understanding of flatpicking and your knowledge of the guitar if you take the extra time and effort. All of the examples, charts, and tunes are numbered sequentially for clarity in the text and on the tape. (For example, Chart 3 follows Example 2 even though there is no Chart 1 or 2.)

As you work with this book and tape, keep track of your progress, questions, thoughts, licks, and solos in a spiral-bound music notebook. Get in the habit of writing music down, whether it's standard notation or some type of tablature. Sure, it'll be tough going at first, but it'll help you keep track of where you're going and where you've been. An added plus is that in the process you'll learn to write down your music whether in tab or standard notation.

A metronome is a great tool for learning new tunes, techniques, and, most importantly, timing. It takes a while to learn how to work with one, especially if you're just beginning to play the guitar. Still, the results make it worth the effort. Don't give up if you can't play along the first few times.

Start out playing a melody or rhythm part at a very slow metronome speed. As you progress, gradually increase speed. Record your progress in the notebook. Always work at speeds that slightly challenge you; but remember, if you can't play it slowly, you surely can't play it fast. Set a target speed and work up to it gradually. Most of these tunes have a wide range of possible tempos. For this reason I haven't listed specific metronome settings on the tunes.

Taped rhythm sections can add a more realistic band context to your practicing. They allow you to play along on a tune, solo, or rhythm part hundreds of times until you get it just right. Make your own on cassette with a guitar and metronome or check out my *BackUp Trax* with a string rhythm section (guitar, bass, and mandolin). We never get tired! We'll pick with you until the cows come home.

For those of you who are more advanced flatpickers (especially after you've nailed down everything in this book!), we have an *Advanced Flatpicking Handbook* and tape nearly completed. It will discuss advanced and hot lead picking, fiddle tunes, cross picking, double stops, open ring solos, music theory, tips on how to improvise, and much more. Watch for it.

Footnotes can be found at the end of this book on page 104.

If you have any comments or questions on the *Beginning Country Guitar Handbook* or *BackUp Trax* book-and-tape sets, please write: Dix Bruce, c/o Musix, P.O. Box 231005, Pleasant Hill, CA 94523.

Shall we proceed?

# Rhythm

Let's begin with accompaniment chords and basic backup rhythm.

4/4 and 3/4 are the most common meters or time signatures found in bluegrass and country music. There are others, such as 2/4, 3/8, and 6/8, but for our purposes we'll look at them as variations of the two basics.

In 4/4 we divide the measure into four equal parts and think, sing, tap our feet, or clap our hands to "one, two, three, four" for every measure. In 3/4, or waltz time, we have "one, two, three" per measure.

Within the measure we divide beats into **"downbeats"** and **"backbeats."** In 4/4 the downbeats are on beats one and three, backbeats are on two and four. In 3/4 beat one is the downbeat, two and three the backbeats. The first measure of Exercise 5, diagrammed with beat numbers, downbeats and backbeats, is below.

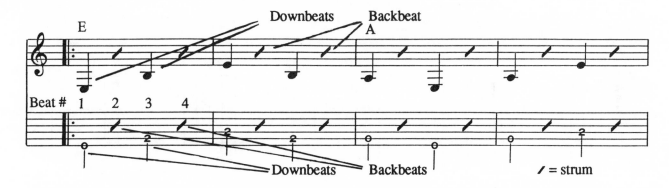

In flatpick rhythm we pick a bass note on each downbeat and strum a chord on each backbeat. The backbeats give the whole measure its "groove," so don't be shy about playing them out. The ultimate effect of this punch on the backbeats is a kind of "one, *two*, three, *four*" in 4/4 feel and "one, *two, three*, one, *two, three*" in 3/4.

You'll notice in the first exercises, and in virtually all flatpicking backup, that the "root tone," or "one"[1] of the chord is always played on the first downbeat. (In the case of an A chord, this will be an A bass note, fifth string open.) "Root" and "one" are interchangeable terms. The root is followed by a strum (or two strums if you are in 3/4). The next downbeat is most often the "five" of whatever chord you are playing but can also be the "three," as with the G chord. (See Chart 3.) This is again followed by a strum or strums. In 3/4 our second bass note, the "five" or "three" of the chord, will be on the first beat of the next measure followed again by two strums. See the first measure of Exercise 5 below. On some chords there are two choices an octave apart for the root or the five, as with the A and E chords. Try alternating them.

The numbers below the chord diagrams in Chart 3 show what part of the chord each string supplies. Make sure that you can maintain a simple "root-strum-five (or three)-strum" rhythm on all the chords shown before you try the exercises that follow. In some cases, like the C, F, and B♭ chords, you'll need to move a finger to fret the five bass note. The diagrams for these chords have a broken circle on the fret you need to move to. Use the closest adjacent finger. (Some people hold both the root and five continually, but I find that the finger change makes for a better rhythmic feel by cutting off the ring of the root while moving to the five.) In the first few exercises and tunes you'll see a small "M" where a finger move occurs. The last part of

Exercise 5 will give you practice on these moves. Notice that the first and sixth strings will provide the same part of the chord when fretted. That's because they're both E notes, although string one is two octaves higher than string six.

# Chart 3

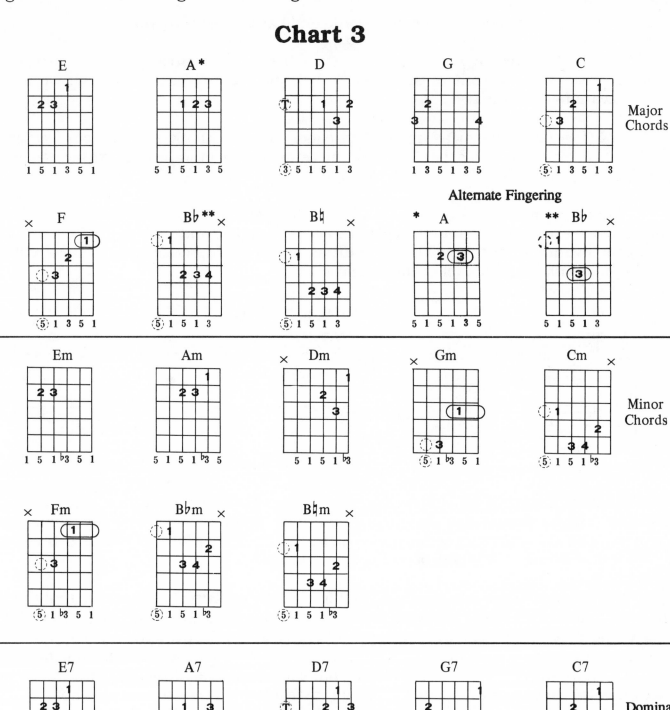

Major Chords

Alternate Fingering

Minor Chords

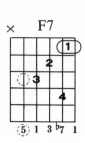
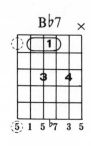
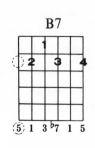

Dominant Seven Chords

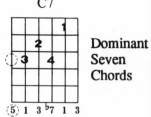

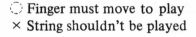
◯ Finger must move to play
× String shouldn't be played

10

Practice all the exercises using a single downstrum and then a down-up strum. Both are demonstrated on the tape, Exercise 4. Most of the exercises and tunes show strums as slashes (/). In some cases specific strum directions are indicated as arrows: downstroke (↓) and upstroke (↑).

For an extra challenge, play through the exercises a second time and change each major chord to minor, each minor to major. Bass notes, as long as they are the one and five of the chord, are the same for major and minor chords of the same name. (To change a major chord to a minor chord, we lower the third of the major chord one half step.) Dominant-seven (e.g., D7, G7, B♭7) and minor-seven chords (e.g., Em7, Am7, E♭m7) use the same bass notes as their major and minor cousins respectively. You should also begin making up your own exercises and songs based on your weaknesses — anything to help teach your fingers to play what you want them to play. For general practice, get a few bluegrass and folk songbooks and work your way through all the songs using bass-strum backup. The bibliography at the end of this book lists several good sources.

★     ★     ★     ★     ★     ★     ★     ★

While you practice and memorize each chord and its bass notes, remember that strums will not necessarily include all six strings. If you've picked a bass note on the sixth string, your strum will generally be on strings five through one. You won't play the sixth string again as part of your strum, but you will let the bass note ring with the following strum. If you pick a bass note on the fourth string, your strum will be on strings three through one and so on. However, you can achieve different rhythmic effects by strumming more or fewer strings.

Upstrums are usually played on only the first two or three strings. All strums serve the double purpose of reinforcing the harmony of the song's chords while defining its rhythmic pulse. In different situations you might emphasize the rhythmic over the harmonic function, or vice versa, by clipping the chords or by letting them ring. Practice both. This symbol / denotes a strum over the chord-note strings; this ✗ means repeat the previous measure.

I've mostly limited these chord diagrams and exercises to "open-position" chords (chords which include open or non-fretted strings), which are the chords most commonly found in bluegrass and country music. Barre chords are certainly indispensable for any serious guitarist, but they are beyond the scope of this handbook. B♭m, Bm, and Cm are closed-position exceptions all played with the same fretting-hand position moved up or down the neck. Remember: Work on the difficult parts, not the easy ones!

Exercise 5 will help you practice bass notes and strums for all the common major, minor, and dominant-seven chords. You'll need to develop the ability to play this "bass-strum" backup rhythm smoothly over all the chords without missing bass notes or strums.

To keep the exercises simple and easy to play, I left out bass/five-finger moves on the chords like C, F, Gm, etc., in the major and minor sections. You'll get to them in the dominant-seven section. As such, some of the bass notes you'll play in these first two sections will not be on the bass strings of the guitar. For now, that's fine; but, as a general rule, keep the bass notes on the bottom three strings.

It's usually quite clear which fretting finger you'll need to move to get to your lower-five bass note. I almost always use the same finger with which I fretted the root. So, on the C chord, I move my third finger from the fifth string, 3rd fret, to the sixth string, 3rd fret. If I had to state a rule, I'd say use the closest finger adjacent to the fret you are moving to. Once you can comfortably play the finger moves in the dominant-seven section, go back to the major and minor sections and try putting in finger moves in the second measure of the C, F, B♭, and B chords.

Exercise 5 will also drill you on what I consider to be the most important component of good music — **rhythm.** If the rhythm is bad, forget the rest. It won't matter how fast you can pick leads, how good you can sing, or how much your herringbone D-28 guitar cost. Good rhythm gives players and listeners alike something basic to relate to. It's difficult to describe in words, but it is something to "groove" and sway to, totally sensual, non-intellectual, non-verbal. Of course it's subjective on any level, and the development of perfect time is not necessarily the goal. As you progress you'll develop your own internal sense of rhythm and groove, which may change according to the different situations and players you experience. You'll learn what other players need from you and what you need from them. Train yourself by studying the greats and analyzing what it is about their music that moves you. This "bass-strum" technique, also called basic "Carter" style after Mother Maybelle Carter's playing, is the mother of virtually all bluegrass and country guitar. Spend a great deal of time on it and you'll build a solid foundation for the lead and more intricate techniques that follow.

# Exercise 4

# Exercise 5

13

Chart 6 shows all the chords of each key based on the major scale. You can also use it to determine the major scales by ignoring the chord symbols (m, o) and reading horizontally. We can see that the G major scale (1–8) is G, A, B, C, D, E, F♯, and G again. If we read across with the chord symbols we find that the chords in the key of G (I-vii°, VIII would be G major again) are G major, A minor, B minor, C major, D major, E minor, and F♯ diminished. (Arabic numerals are used to identify scale notes, Roman numerals identify chords.) Since you have the recipes of the chords listed above, you can figure out which notes make up any given chord. What notes are in the Gm7 chord? The B♭7? The E♭m7?

# Chart 6

| | | Numbers: | 1 | 2 | 3 | 4 | 5 | 6 | 7 | 8 |
|---|---|---|---|---|---|---|---|---|---|---|
| | | Scale | | | | | | | | |
| Key | ♯/♭ | Chord | I | ii | iii | IV | V | vi | viio | VIII |
| C | none | | C | Dm | Em | F | G | Am | Bo | C |
| F | 1♭ | | F | Gm | Am | B♭ | C | Dm | Eo | F |
| B♭ | 2♭ | | B♭ | Cm | Dm | E♭ | F | Gm | Ao | B♭ |
| E♭ | 3♭ | | E♭ | Fm | Gm | A♭ | B♭ | Cm | Do | E♭ |
| A♭ | 4♭ | | A♭ | B♭m | Cm | D♭ | E♭ | Fm | Go | A♭ |
| D♭ | 5♭ | | D♭ | E♭m | Fm | G♭ | A♭ | B♭m | Co | D♭ |
| G♭ | 6♭ | | G♭ | A♭m | B♭m | C♭ | D♭ | E♭m | Fo | G♭ |
| C♭ | 7♭ | | C♭ | D♭m | E♭m | F♭ | G♭ | A♭m | B♭o | C♭ |
| C♯ | 7♯ | | C♯ | D♯m | E♯m | F♯ | G♯ | A♯m | B♯o | C♯ |
| F♯ | 6♯ | | F♯ | G♯m | A♯m | B | C♯ | D♯m | E♯o | F♯ |
| B | 5♯ | | B | C♯m | D♯m | E | F♯ | G♯m | A♯o | B |
| E | 4♯ | | E | F♯m | G♯m | A | B | C♯m | D♯o | E |
| A | 3♯ | | A | B♯m | C♯m | D | E | F♯m | G♯o | A |
| D | 2♯ | | D | Em | F♯m | G | A | Bm | C♯o | D |
| G | 1♯ | | G | Am | Bm | C | D | Em | F♯o | G |

**Note:** Some of the keys are listed with two different *enharmonic* names. For example, G♭ and F♯, C♭ and B, and D♭ and C♯ are enharmonic names for the same key.

17

# Connecting Notes

Bluegrass and country guitarists rarely play as sparsely as in Exercise 5. Usually they punctuate their playing with connecting notes and bass runs. **Connecting notes** are used to connect chords. Exercise 7 explores some possibilities in both 4/4 and 3/4 time. You can use these notes to connect chords in any tune or song. Switches from major to minor may not work because connecting notes from one chord may not be in the chord or scale of the other.

For example, you might use the descending notes D-C#-B to go from a D major chord to an A major. The C# may sound strange in the connecting run to A minor, since the A minor chord does not have a C# note in its scale. Rather, it has a C natural. A general rule is to play the run in the scale of the chord you are approaching.

As you play Exercise 7, and virtually every other piece in this book, be sure to keep your fretting hand in the basic position of the chord. Don't release the chord to grab a bass or connecting note unless you absolutely have to. Since the basic flatpicking style requires playing both lead and rhythm simultaneously, any unnecessary hand motion will work against you. The trick is to smoothly integrate one with the other. In the 4/4 exercise, I marked the bass/five-finger moves. You'll be able find them yourself in the 3/4 exercise and from now on. Again, challenge yourself by switching major to minor, single to down-up strum, etc., and by making up your own exercises. I have marked suggested fingerings (circled numbers above standard staff) at points that might not be immediately clear. Throughout this book you'll find these noted the first time a given phrase/position occurs.

## Exercise 7

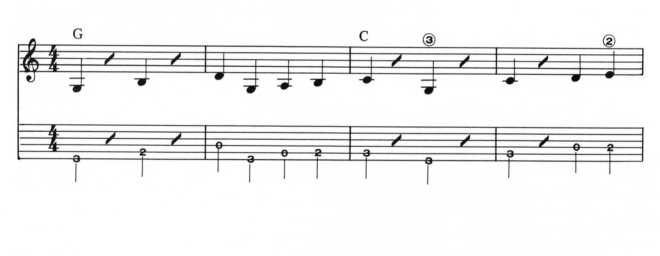

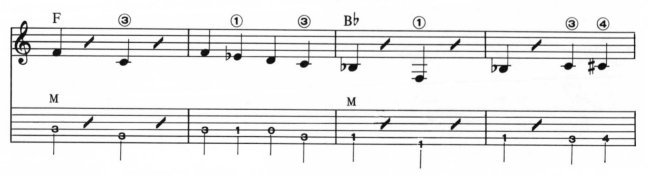

19

20

23

# "Worried Man Blues" and Transposition

**"Worried Man Blues,"** an old Carter Family song, illustrates the basic backup principles you've been practicing. The first half or chorus of the piece is straight "bass-strum" backup with no connecting runs. Again you'll notice the bass notes on the downbeats, the strums on the backbeats. Use both single and then double strums. Mix them in your backup as most guitarists do. Work for an even, controlled feel on both the bass notes and the strums. You may find that you naturally give the backbeats (strums) a bit more accent or volume. Just make sure they don't overpower the bass notes. Notice that the bass notes on this G chord are the root (sixth string, 3rd fret) and the three (fifth string, 2nd fret) rather than the root and the five. The C chords in measures 5 and 17 require a finger move to play the root-five pattern. (To make sure that your measure count is the same as mine, start counting *after* the two-measure introduction where the lyric says "takes.")

The verse adds some possibilities for connecting the chords with bass runs. Keep the timing even and straight. Jump right in and try your own licks, too, and don't forget to write them down!

Be sure to play through all the verses to **"Worried Man Blues."** Practice it until you don't have to think about it. Keep in mind that you're not just memorizing one tune, you're working on the basic moves you'll need for *every* song you play in this style. If you aren't already getting together and jamming with other players, start today! You'll learn much more quickly by sharing. Work with the tape. Singing along while you play will also make it a lot more fun. Don't be shy — nobody has to hear but you!

Look ahead in this book and try to play all the songs with the backup techniques you've already learned. Each time you learn a new concept, go through the book again and try it on all the other tunes.

### Additional lyrics:

I went across the river and I laid down to sleep (three times)
When I awoke, I had shackles on my feet.

Twenty-nine links of chain around my leg
And on each link an initial of my name.

I asked the judge, "What might be my fine?"
"Twenty-one years on the Rocky Mountain Line."

If anyone should ask you who composed this song
Tell 'em 'twas I and I sing it all day long.

# Tune 8: "Worried Man Blues"

# Capos

As many of you know, a **capo** is a clamp that can be positioned on the guitar neck to effectively "shorten" the length of the strings. We place the capo in any fret, slightly behind the metal fretwire, adjust it until there's a minimum of buzzes and rattles, and play. The resulting chord or note will sound higher than the same thing played without the capo. If an E chord is played with the capo clamped on the 3rd fret, the resulting *sound* will be a G chord, even though the player is holding what looks like an E chord. Each fret is equal to one half step. Since in this case the capo is 3 frets above the guitar nut, the resulting chord is three half steps above the standard E. If the capo were on the 4th fret, the resulting chord would become G♯ or A♭.

To determine the new chord, note, or key in a capoed position, count up by half steps the number of frets you capo up. The chromatic (half step) scale is: C, C♯/D♭, D, D♯/E♭, E, F, F♯/G♭, G, G♯/A♭, A, A♯/B♭, B, C — 12 different notes in all. Notes listed with a slash, like C♯/D♭, are different names — **"enharmonic spellings"** — for the same note. You can call it by either name. Suppose you play a G chord capoed up 5 frets. The resulting sound will be a C chord. What would a G chord be capoed up 6 frets? How about an A chord capoed up 1 fret?

The practical advantage of the capo is that a guitarist can learn a tune's melody or chord progression in one key and then, by correctly positioning the capo, play that melody or chord progression in several different keys without re-learning it. In this way you can accommodate other singers and players who perform a tune in a different key than you know.

The capo can be an artistic tool, as well. Play an open B♭ chord. Now capo at the 3rd fret and play a G chord, which is now really a B♭. Notice how different they sound? You may prefer one over the other for a particular effect on a tune. (If you're a beginner, you may find it much easier to play the capoed G than the regular B♭ chord.) When two guitarists work together, one can play open chords while the other plays capoed up. The result is a very full sound. For example, one could play an open C while the other played a G capoed at the 5th fret.

Capos do have their drawbacks. One is that when moved they usually require you to retune the guitar. I've used just about every type of capo on the market: elastic straps, spring clamps, thumb screw clamps, etc., and they all send your tuning out of whack. That can be a pain in the neck, especially for your audience — if you're on stage and switching positions a lot, you'll spend more time tuning than playing. Another drawback is that capos can become a crutch and a roadblock to learning transposition theory. For now, learn to play tunes in other open keys before you "capo up." You'll find your general guitar knowledge will develop far more quickly than if you just slap on the capo. Learn what's really involved in transposing first. We'll get into it a bit deeper in **"Late Last Night,"** but first let's work on a transposing and capo exercise.

★    ★    ★    ★    ★    ★    ★    ★

**"Worried Man Blues"** is written here in the key of G. Let's assume that we need to play it for our singer in the key of D. Consult Chart 6 [2] on page 17 to convert the chords from the key of G to the key of D. Go to the horizontal line of the key you're playing in — in this case the key of G. Within that line find the first chord, G. Follow up or down in that column to the desired *new* key — in this case D — and play the corresponding chord. All the G chords become Ds, the Cs become Gs, and the Ds become As. Write these transposed chords in pencil over the given chords, and play the song in the new key of D. Chart 3 on page 10 will refresh your memory if you've forgotten the chord fingerings or their bass notes. By using Chart 6 in this way, you can play **"Worried Man Blues"** in any of the 12 keys. Look ahead in this book and transpose each of the other tunes to a different key. This will give you great practice in transposing, and the alternate-key playing will build up your backup repertoire. The process will help you memorize the relationships between notes and chords in keys. Soon you'll do it easily from memory, without the chart.

Let's get back to our singer. Now he (she) wants to sing **"Worried Man Blues"** one half step higher, in the key of E♭! First we look at Chart 6 and transpose from the key of D to the key of E♭. D chords become E♭ chords, Gs become A♭s, and As become B♭s. No problem. Well, maybe one slight problem, especially if you're a beginner. Those new chords are tough to finger and don't easily lend themselves to the bass-strum style we need for backup. No problem, here's where the capo really does its stuff. Since we need to play the key-of-D chords one half step higher in the key of E♭, we can simply place the capo in the 1st fret and play the song with the key-of-D chords. The resulting capoed *sound* will be one half step higher in the key of E♭. Again, look ahead in the book and try capoing each of the tunes to another place on your guitar. What's the highest fret in which you can comfortably use the capo? Where do you find special tuning problems?

Wait! The singer's not through yet. He (she) has decided to play the guitar, too, and wants you to capo in a different position. No problem. We already know that we can transpose **"Worried Man Blues"** to any of 12 different keys and that any of those can be moved up the neck with a capo. Our task is to find the right combination of chords and capo to keep us in the key of E♭. Key-of-D chords capoed at the 1st fret are one possibility, but our singer wants to play those. All we need to do is go back to Chart 6 and pick another key to transpose to.

First go back to the original key of G. How can we play G-key chords and have them sound like E♭? Count from G up to E♭ chromatically — G, A♭, A, B♭, B, C, D♭, D, E♭. It's an interval of 8 half steps or frets. Place the capo in the 8th fret and play the G-key chords. Suppose we want to play C-key chords? Count 3 half steps or frets from C to E♭. Try this for as many chords and keys as you can think of on all the tunes in this book. With practice these types of transpositions will become second nature.

# Bass Runs

Once you've mastered the basics of the chords, bass notes, connecting notes and strums, you'll probably be eager to add in a bit more spice to your backup. By listening to any good bluegrass or country guitarist, you'll notice extra little licks or runs punctuating the vocal or instrumental melody line. These are **bass runs.** The most basic (Ex. 9, #1) is generally known as the "Lester Flatt G run." Guess why.... That's right, Lester Flatt popularized it while playing with Bill Monroe and later in his band with Earl Scruggs. Exercise 9 has several variations. This will be your first experience playing eighth notes, which necessitate up-and-down picking. We'll discuss this more when we get to **Straight Lead Picking** on page 68. For now follow the suggested pick directions: ↓ for a downstroke, ↑ for an upstroke. Numbers 4, 5, and 6 have hammer-ons. If you're unfamiliar with hammer-ons, hang on. We'll get to them next.

It's very important to memorize these runs and learn them in other open (no-capo) keys. Although these particular runs are not used as often in minor keys, you should once again try to switch them from major to minor keys. Some of the runs shown end in strums, some whole notes. Consider them interchangeable. Obviously, there are hundreds of other possibilities for bass runs.

The second part of Exercise 9 shows a few of the runs converted from 4/4 to 3/4 time. Figure out the rest and write them down in your notebook. This will give you practice in forming your own new licks from ones you already know. All I did was stretch the runs from two to four measures and add extra strums. You can also delete strums to make a two-measure 3/4 run.

## Exercise 9

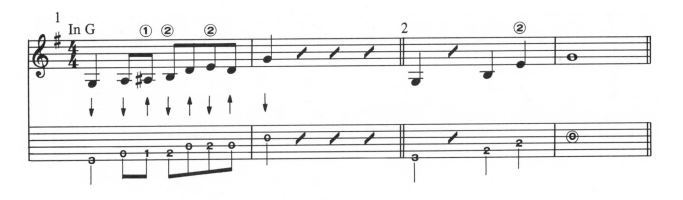

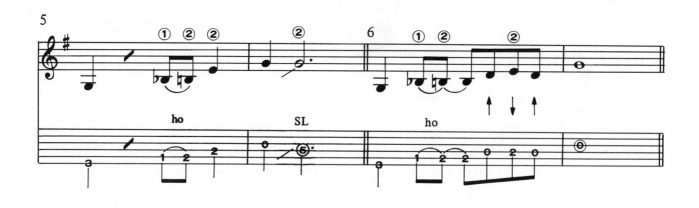

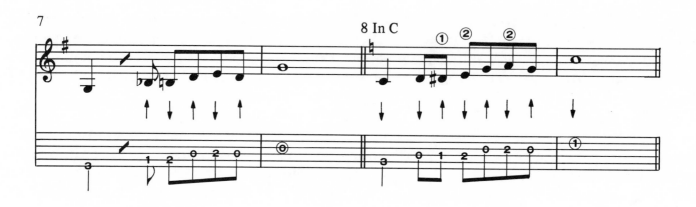

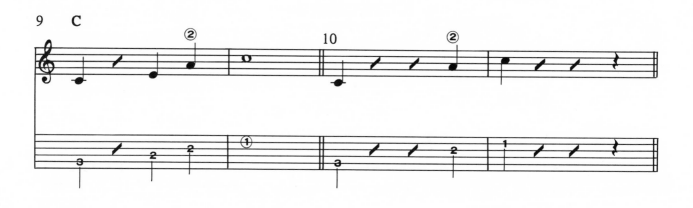

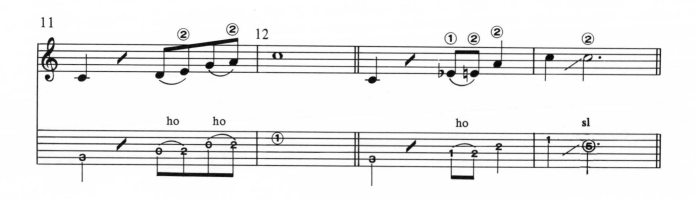

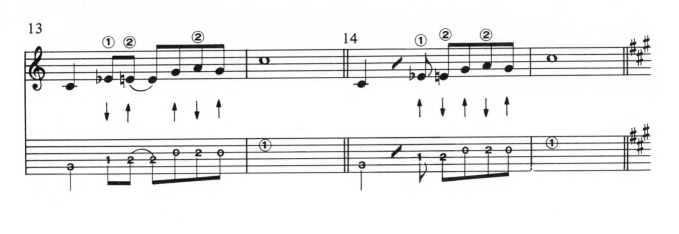

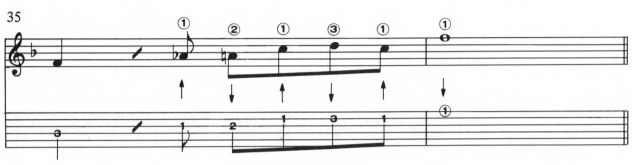

**Runs in ¾**

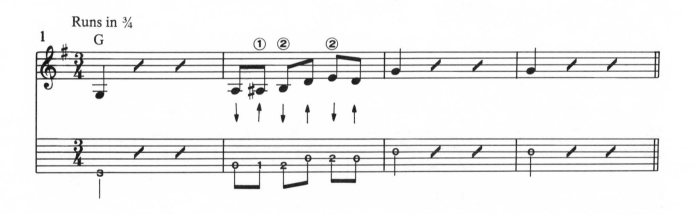

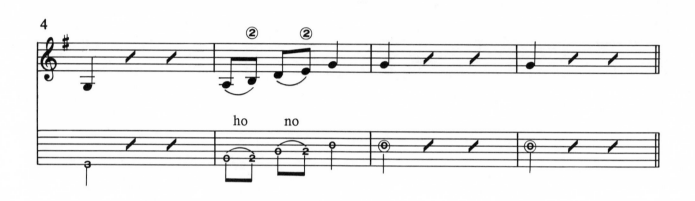

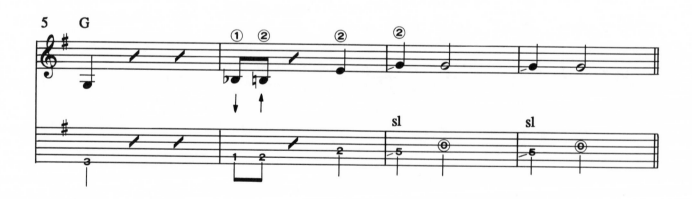

Another exercise that will help you expand your repertoire of runs is to invert them. It's easy — you just play a lick backwards. I often move it up an octave. Of course, if you move the new lick up an octave, it might not be a "bass" run any longer; but that's OK. Look at Example 9a. I took bass runs #1 and #21 and played them backwards! Then I moved each up an octave. You don't need to invert exactly, but experiment with all the runs shown in Exercise 9. You can make use of this inversion technique later when you study lead improvisation.

# Exercise 9a

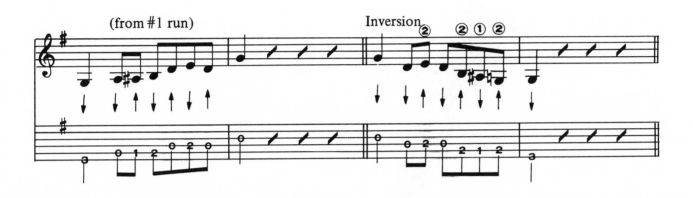

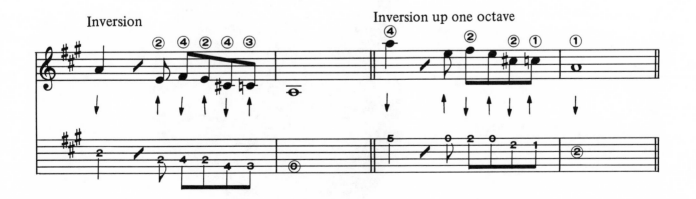

Listen to one of the recordings below and identify and learn four or five bass runs. Change the runs I've listed to fit your own ideas. If you find yourself overwhelmed by the number of runs you're working with, take a couple of favorites and place them in the context of a song. Each time you play the song, play the chosen licks in the same place. This will help you integrate them directly into your playing. Later on (page 58) you'll learn how to construct a solo using only these types of runs.

Just about any Original Carter Family, Norman Blake, Doc Watson, Dan Crary, or Tony Rice record is packed with ideas. I especially like Norman and Tony's *Blake & Rice* (Rounder 0233) and Tony and Ricky Skaggs' *Skaggs and Rice* (Sugar Hill 3711). Both duo recordings, they show great backup (and lead!) guitar with wonderful clarity.

# Backup: "Swing Low, Sweet Chariot"

Each of the techniques you've worked on so far is a part of the overall skill of playing rhythm or backup. Those of you who aspire to be great *lead* flatpickers might downplay the importance of backup playing — who ever notices it? Audiences never applaud the "rhythm" players!

It is a subtle skill —an art at its best — but you'll find that it's more important than just about anything else in music. If the backup is lousy, the finest vocal or lead work will be lost in a swamp of bad time, wrong chords, poorly chosen runs, and awful grooves. Listen to what the great players do with their backup. Listen especially to what they leave out. Take the time to learn the mechanics of good rhythm playing. It's the foundation from which you'll build your more advanced playing.

Here's a complete backup chart to **"Swing Low, Sweet Chariot."** If you find the connecting and bass runs too difficult, leave them out at first and just do the "bass-strum" backup. The tune ends with a full G run, but you'll find several other "partials" punctuating the lyrics throughout. Once you get the feel of them, substitute others, including inverted runs, from Exercise 9. Extra lyrics are below.

**Additional lyrics:**

Well I looked over Jordan and what did I see?
Coming for to carry me home. (repeated after each line)
A band of angels coming after me
Coming for to carry me home.

Sometimes I'm up, Lord sometimes I'm down
(Coming etc.)
One thing I know I'm heavenly bound

If you get to heaven before I do
Tell all my friends I'm coming there too

# Tune 10: "Swing Low, Sweet Chariot"

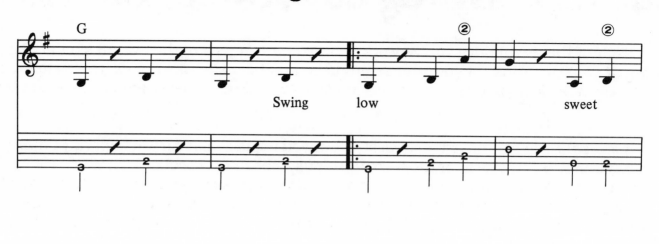

Swing  low                    sweet

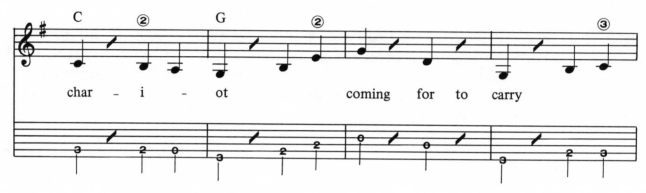

char – i – ot        coming  for  to  carry

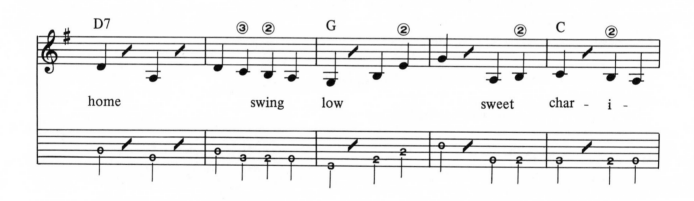

home           swing   low        sweet   char – i –

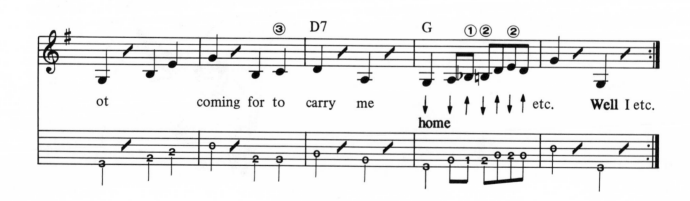

ot        coming for to  carry  me        ↓ ↓ ↑ ↓ ↑ ↓ ↑ etc.        Well I etc.

home

As you can see, there really isn't much more to backup than "bass-strum, bass-strum" and a few licks. Of course you need to learn how to play solid and inspiring time that doesn't speed up or slow down. Beyond that it's all feel and groove. That's the tough part! You won't develop it intellectually — you have to play and listen and play some more.

The first step is to work on the bass-strum technique until it's second nature, until you can do it with all the chords, without lapses, in your sleep. Have you been looking ahead in the book and playing basic backup to all the other songs? If not, you should take the time to do it now and make it a regular part of your practice routine. Spend a good deal of time, weeks or even months, just playing simple backup. If it's boring, you're missing the whole point. Internalize it and make it a musical end in and of itself.

Memorize the chord progressions to the tunes you're working with. You won't be able to concentrate on the rhythmic flow if you're searching for chords on a page. Memorization will also help you hear the patterns that chords in songs typically follow. And, the more you practice memorization, the easier it will become. Practice will make perfect, or at least better!

Play backup rhythm along with the accompanying tape. Start by listening to both lead and rhythm. Try to *groove* with the track without speeding up, slowing down, or stopping. Then listen to and play with only the rhythm side. In recording it, I kept it very simple with a minimum of bass notes and runs so you can add your own. Finally, listen to and play along with the lead only.

Play as much as possible with others. My *Backup Trax Fiddle Tunes* tape set might come in handy now, especially if you're not part of a regular jam session. It lets you play along with a variety of tunes four and five times through, which builds strength, stamina, and confidence.

# Hammer-Ons and Pull-Offs

**Hammer-ons** and **pull-offs** are widely used flatpick techniques. To play them, you pick a note and then, while it is still ringing, "hammer on" or "pull off" with a fretting finger and, hopefully, the picked string will continue to ring and sound the new note. Hammers go from a lower to a higher note; pulls go from higher to lower. Most hammers can be reversed to be pulls and vice versa. Don't forget to reverse all of them.

Look at the first line of Example 11 below. Hold a standard Em chord. Pick the open A (fifth) string and quickly fret the B note on the same string. Practice until both the open A and fretted B notes ring equally well. This may take a bit of practice until the buzzes are eliminated, so don't give up. Try the C-chord example.

A pull-off is the reverse of a hammer-on. Hold the Em and pick the fretted E note (fourth string). Quickly move your fretting finger off the E note and let the open D ring. (The action is probably more of a "push" than a "pull.") I usually push off in the direction of the ceiling, rather than toward the floor. If I'm on the first string, I'll go either way. Again, don't expect it to work perfectly the first time. The next pull-off begins with a third-string A. Move the finger you used on the fourth string over to catch the third string, 2nd fret. Pick the A note and pull off to the G.

Both of these examples of hammers and pulls start or end on open strings. They can also be used between two fretted notes. Hammers and pulls are identified in the music with slur markings: ⌣ or ⌢ or the designations "ho" and "po" for hammer-on and pull-off respectively.

Both are written in one of two ways, as two notes slurred 🎵 or as one note with a slur-type marking ♪ . The latter denotes a hammer from an open to a fretted string.

I generally give the two-note version a more pronounced, two-note feel. The one-note slur gets a faster hammer or pull and is treated more as a "grace" note.

Hammers & Pulls Basic Example     **Example 11**

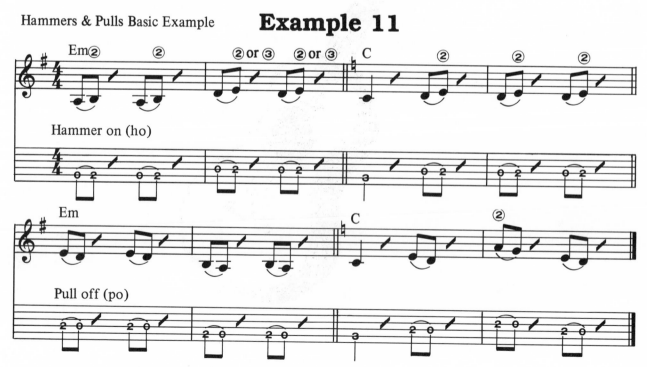

Hammer on (ho)

Pull off (po)

Exercise 12 will help you develop facility in playing hammer-ons and pull-offs. Once you feel comfortable with 12, try the backup to **"Midnight Special"** first in the key of E with hammers and then in the key of G with pulls. You probably wouldn't play hammers or pulls constantly throughout a song as written here. Use your judgment as you apply the techniques to other songs.

Also go back to Exercise 5 on page 12 and use the hammers and pulls on bass notes of your bass-strum patterns where possible. Look ahead in the book and try them on other songs.

# Exercise 12

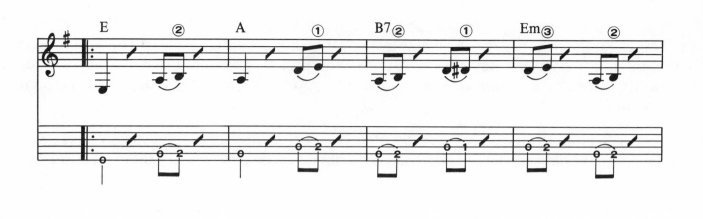

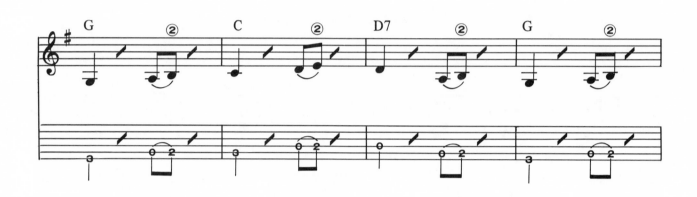

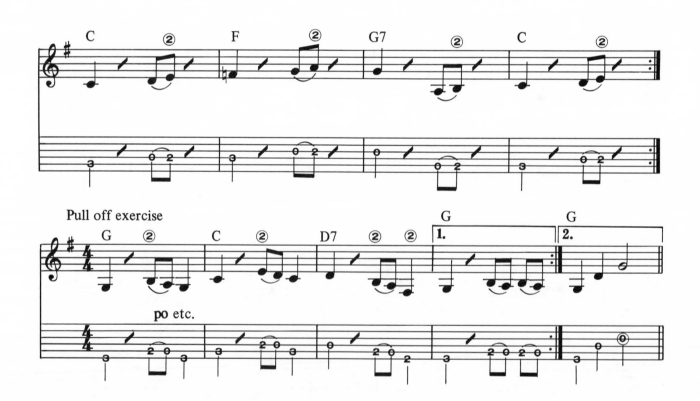

Pull off exercise

po etc.

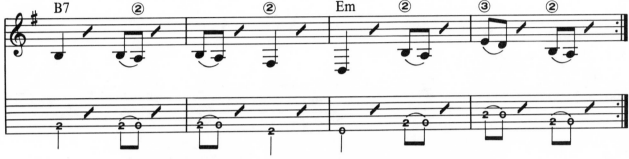

## Tune 12a: "Midnight Special"

Hammer section in E

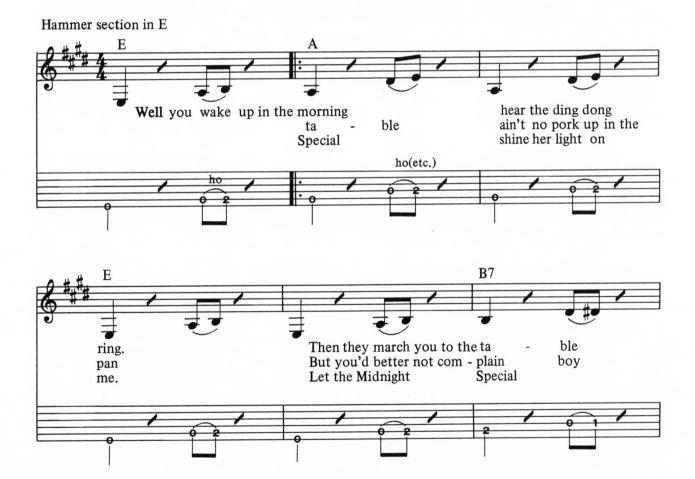

Well you wake up in the morning
ta - ble
Special

hear the ding dong
ain't no pork up in the
shine her light on

ho(etc.)

ring.
pan
me.

Then they march you to the ta - ble
But you'd better not com - plain boy
Let the Midnight Special

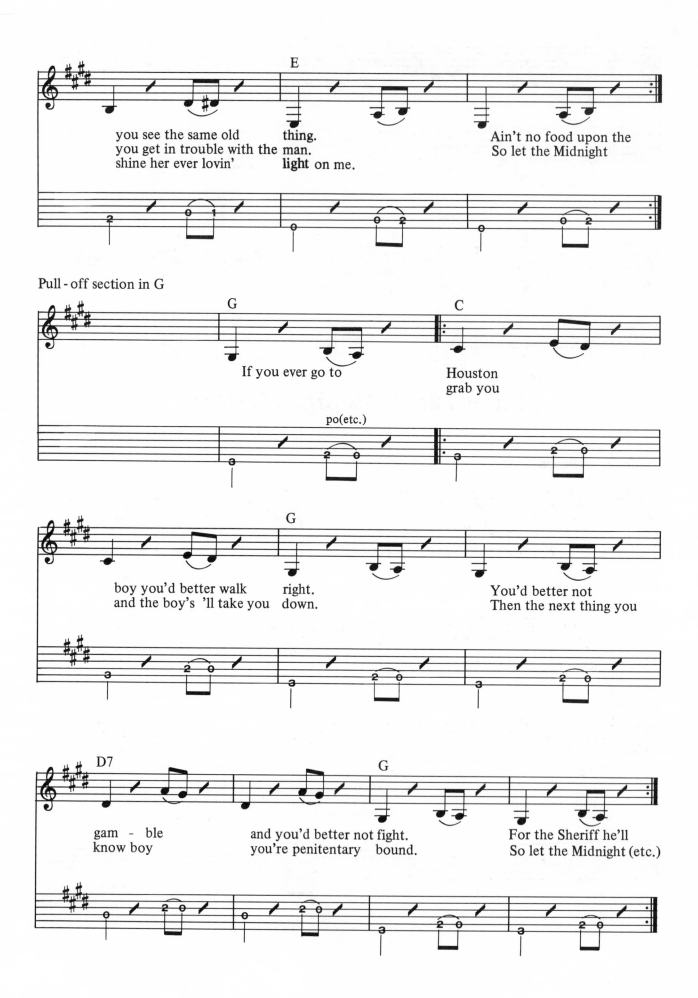

Pull-off section in G

# "Late Last Night"

On the first half of **"Late Last Night,"** you'll practice hammers, pulls, single and double brushes. It's written in basic "Carter style," where simple melodic phrases are incorporated into the guitar rhythm. This technique is a bridge between straight backup and straight lead playing and represents a mixture of both. It's especially useful in small groups where the guitar plays a vital rhythmic role. Carter picking keeps the rhythm going while the lead melody is floated over it.

Notice the eighth-note variations in measures 12 and 14. These are added to give variety to the melody. Follow the suggested pick-direction arrows. The general rule (covered in greater depth in the **Straight Lead Picking** section) is to use downstrokes on beats 1, 2, 3, 4, and upstrokes on "ands" in between the beats (1 *and* 2 *and* 3 *and* 4 *and*). You'll find yourself adding your own variations as you learn this and other tunes and perform them again and again. (When counting measures, start after the three-note introduction. Measure 1 is immediately to the right of the first double bar.)

The second half is a slightly more difficult melody with more eighth notes and melodic variations added. It's an extension or development of the first. Use the first half as a statement of the song's melody, the second as a flatpicking solo. Your hand should stay in each basic chord position while you pick, since all the notes are within reach. Not only will this conservation of movement help you play more smoothly and ultimately faster, it'll also help you transpose **"Late Last Night"** to other keys.

## Tune 13: "Late Last Night"

45

he was    slippin'    and a -    slidin'    with his    new    shoes
It's       oh                      me       and it's     oh
with       one arm   a -         round     my          old        gui -
Well I    brought nothing        with me    in - to     this old

on         Papa said,  "Willie   don't you   rap        no         more."
my         ain't got    no one    to          go         my         bail.
tar        and the     other arm  a -         round      my         dear.
world      ain't gonna take       nothing     to         my         grave.

**Solo**

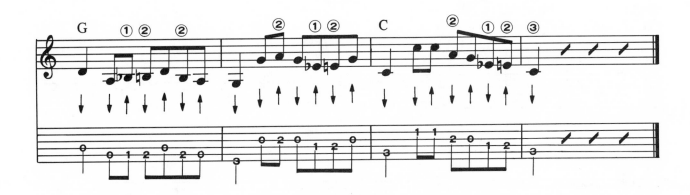

Once you've committed the tune to memory, try transposing it to the key of G. The first few bars are shown, and they'll help you get started. If you get hung up, refer to the key-of-C version and Chart 6 on page 17. Try to think of it as moving what you played in the key of C over one string — down in pitch for the G version, up in pitch for the F version. Keep your fretting hand in the basic G-chord position as I mentioned, and you'll find it quite simple. Write it all down in your notebook.

The key-of-A version is quite different — it doesn't lie on the neck with the same symmetry as C and G — although not that difficult. Again you'll find the first few bars shown. Try all the keys you can think of. Don't use the capo on this tune until you can transpose without it.

# Example 14

# Slides

**Slides,** both ascending and descending, are somewhat similar to hammers and pulls in both technique and sound. The difference is that, instead of putting a finger down or picking it up to sound the second note, you pick the first note and slide the fretting finger up or down to the second note without damping the sound. Guitarists of every style use this basic technique and add variations according to the particular sounds they want. You can slide between two fretted or one open and one fretted note.

Slides are shown in music with slurs ♪ , just like hammers and pulls, as well as with the symbol "sl." If hammers, pulls, or slides aren't specified, it's up to you to decide which you want to use. Go back to Exercise 9 (page 29) and try putting slides into your bass runs. Go back to Exercise 12 (page 41) and swap slides for hammers and pulls.

## Exercise 15

49

# "Corinna"

**"Corinna"** includes basic bass-strum rhythms, runs, slides, hammers and pulls, and lead melody playing. It's written in the key of A and requires a bit more finger stretching than we've used up to this point.

You'll need to use a modified A "barre" chord, noted in the music as A*, in order to fit the strums in smoothly with the lead lines. I use my first finger to fret strings two, three, and four at the 2nd fret. Be careful not to fret the first string — either let it ring open or mute it so that it doesn't sound at all. (The F♯ note would make the chord an A6.) Don't worry too much about clear-ringing strums. This is one of those cases where the strum acts more as a rhythm chop than a harmonic statement. Just make sure that no strings buzz.

Another chord position you might try on both the backup and lead is the "hoe-handle A," as Tony Rice calls it. This form adds an A note on string one, which really rings out. Be forewarned that playing the melody in this position makes for some serious finger stretches.

## Tune 16: "Corinna"

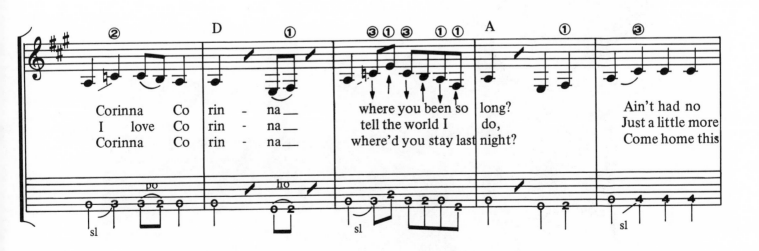

51

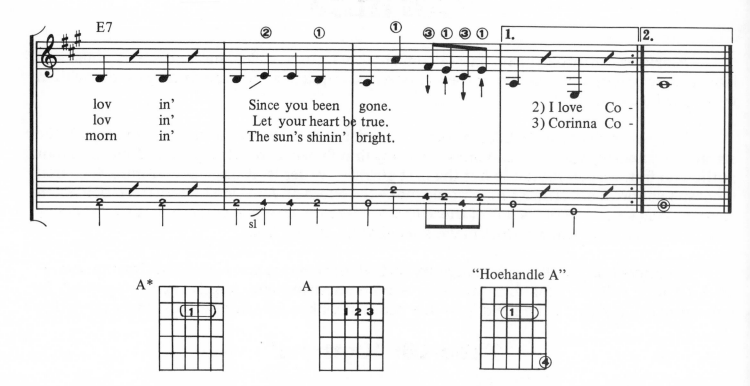

| lov | in' |
|-----|-----|
| lov | in' |
| morn | in' |

Since you been | gone.
Let your heart be true.
The sun's shinin' | bright.

E7

A*     A     "Hoehandle A"

2) I love    Co -
3) Corinna Co -

Once you can play it as written, try it an octave higher in the same position. Your first note will be an E on the fourth string, 2nd fret. Don't worry about playing it exactly — just try to find a recognizable melody without moving your fretting fingers too much.

# "New River Train"

The tunes that we've done so far have featured backup and Carter-style flatpicking. **"New River Train"** demonstrates beginning lead playing on the treble strings and acts as a bridge between backup and exclusive lead playing. Play it first with straight backup including bass strum patterns, connecting runs, and bass runs. On the tape you'll hear the melody played and later sung. The second version has backup, lyrics, and licks to punctuate the vocal of the tune. The effect is a "call and response" between the vocalist and the guitarist. Before you get into these treble-string licks, try fitting bass runs in after each vocal phrase.

Finally, try the "treble" licks shown. These can be plugged into Version 2. The sixth lick shown comes from Ralph Stanley's signature banjo lick; the seventh sounds a bit like a train whistle. Push on the fretted second string to raise its pitch and give the train effect. This string stretch is noted in the music with parentheses: ( ).

It's important that these guitar licks not cover up the vocal but enhance it while filling the space between vocal phrases. You'll hear how they fit together on the tape. This type of call and response is quite common in bluegrass and country music. You could use this approach on songs like **"The Banks of the Ohio," "The Bluebirds Are Singing for Me," "If I Lose," "Crying Holy," "Life Is Like a Mountain Railway," "Nine Pound Hammer,"** and many others. Fit your own bass and treble runs into each of these songs and be sure to try different keys. If you use this technique in a group situation you'll need to share the playing with others. If everyone is listening and cooperating, it should naturally fall together. If it doesn't, you may need to agree beforehand who'll play where. For example, have each player back up the vocal before or after his or her solo.

**"New River Train"** is great for exercising your lyric writing. Meanwhile, here's a few to start with.

**Additional lyrics:**

Darling you can't love two (2 times)
You can't love two and your little heart be true
Darling you can't love two.

Darling you can't love three (2 times)
You can't love three and still love me
Darling you can't love three.

Darling you can't love four (2 times)
You can't love four and love any more
Darling you can't love four, etc.

# Tune 17a: "New River Train" Melody & Backup

I'm riding on that New Riv - er train_____ I'm

riding on that New Riv - er train._____ That

same old train that brought me here's gon - na

car - ry me a - way a - gain.

55

## Tune 17b: "New River Train" with Backup Licks

# Example 18: "New River Train" Backup Licks

Resolves to
G chord

# Generic G-Run Solo

Suppose you're on stage or at a jam session and it's your turn to solo on a tune that you're unfamiliar with. What will you play? **What *will* you play?** How about a generic G-run solo? I've heard guitarists play this type of lead hundreds of times. It's a guaranteed life saver. All you do is play "G-run-like" phrases over the solo space, filling in with extra notes or strums wherever you feel it's necessary. Of course you'll have to transpose the runs to match the chord you are playing over. Minor chords will work, too, and virtually any song can be arranged for a generic solo.

Below are rudimentary examples of solos in three keys: G, D, and C. They can be easily broken into two- and four-measure blocks and used on similar chord changes in other songs. Rearrange and recombine them to fit whatever progression you're working on. After you familiarize yourself with these examples, try the solo below on the chorus chord progression to **"Swing Low, Sweet Chariot"** in the key of G.

Notice that I slightly changed a couple of the runs to make the solo flow a bit better. In the 3rd full measure I ended the C run on a quarter-note A instead of the G that you might have expected. This avoids the necessity of playing two G notes in a row, since the following measure begins on G. In the 11th measure you'll find an F-natural note for variation instead of the D. The F natural leads naturally into the C chord.

After you can play the solo as written, try transposing it to the keys of A, D, and C. All you have to do is substitute the appropriate runs that you're already familiar with.

## Example 19

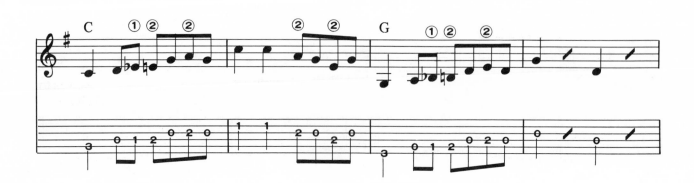

58

# Tune 20: Generic Solo for "Swing Low"

Now make up your own generic solos to tunes we've already covered, like **"Late Last Night"** and **"Worried Man Blues."** Incorporate your own runs. If two identical runs follow each other, invert one. The examples in 19 are written without hammers, pulls, or slides. Don't limit yourself to these rather straight runs — use all the variations you've already studied. Be sure to try writing generic solos to fiddle tunes and 3/4 tunes.

# "Under the Double Eagle"

**"Under the Double Eagle"** is one of the first flatpick leads I learned. I heard it played years ago by Charlie Waller on an early Country Gentlemen record (Folkways FA 2409), and I'm still amazed at how many people of all stylistic interests request or recognize the song at concerts or in rowdy bars. It has saved my life more than once, most recently at a wedding reception when someone requested a polka. My repertoire is a bit lacking in that area, but **"Under the Double Eagle"** worked beautifully. Johnny Gimble recorded it polka-style on his *My Kinda Music* LP (Tejas ST 001).

This arrangement is in the Carter style with single notes and strums mixed. It's written in the key of C, although it's often performed with a modulation to the key of F. This version is much simpler and stays in C. You'll find lots of hammers, and most move from an open-string note to a fretted note. Watch out for the eighth notes, which may trip you up at first in measures 29–30, 41–42 and 45–46. The lick in measure 47 is just a bass run. Measure 41 will give your fretting-hand thumb a workout as you use it to reach around the back of the neck and fret the low F note on the sixth string, 1st fret.

Measures 41–42 have a chord and strum pattern that you may not be familiar with. Check the rhythm out on the tape if you have trouble. The phantom chord is F♯o7 (F sharp diminished seven, usually referred to as just "F sharp diminished").[3] The chord diagram is below the tune. Finally, I've listed a slight variation for the first two measures that you may want to plug in on the repeat. I learned it years ago from Hot Rize's Charles Sawtelle. Don't forget to play **"Under the Double Eagle"** with both single *and* double strums!

# Tune 21: "Under the Double Eagle"

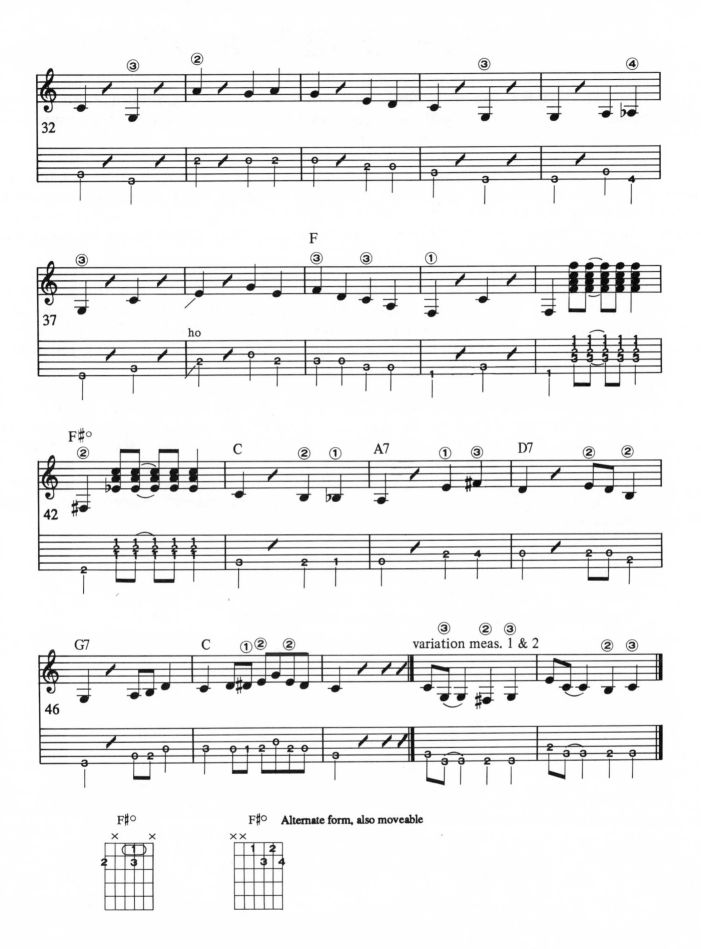

# "I Never Will Marry"

**"I Never Will Marry"** is written in the key of F to give you practice on chords some players seek to avoid. (You know who you are!) After you can play it in F, try it in other keys, especially if the F version is pitched too low or high for your voice.

Lots of finger moves, the first hammer is on the first note. Other hammers follow in measures 13 and 16. The 4th full measure has a pull-off. Measure 16 has a one-two punch where a hammer is immediately followed by a pull-off. Tricky at first, you'll find it an exceptionally useful move, especially for slow songs like this. **"Salt Creek,"** page 78, also uses the hammer-pull technique.

Another useful technique is the **"arpeggiated strum"** in measures 2–4, 6, 10, 11, and 12. Here you strum a chord, letting each individual note sound, and end your strum on a melody note. In measure 2 you strum strings five, four, and end on the open third. Then follow with a regular strum on strings two and one to complete your hand motion. In measure 6 you'll only strum strings four and three for the melody note.

The arpeggiated strum gives you the effect of both rhythm and lead and sounds much fuller than unaccompanied single-string notes. It's great for solo guitarists. Try working out arpeggiated-strum solos to songs like **"Grandfather's Clock," "Columbus Stockade Blues,"** or any other tune you can think of.

Linda Ronstadt recorded a beautiful version of **"I Never Will Marry"** on her *Simple Dreams* LP (Asylum 6E-104). Here's one more verse:

My love's gone and left me, he's the one I adore,
He's gone where I never shall see him no more.
She's plunged her dear body, in the waters so deep,
She closed her pretty blue eyes, in the water to sleep.

# Tune 22: "I Never Will Marry"

# Straight Lead Picking and Exercises

Here's where we get into more advanced flatpicking with eight eighth notes in nearly every measure. Where before we based our playing on "one, two, three, four," we're now thinking "one and two and three and four and." Keep in mind that we're not thinking or playing any faster; rather, we're fitting in eight notes in the same space where we previously had only four.

Pick direction and economy of hand movement are very important. The rule of thumb (so to speak) for pick direction is: Use downstrokes on beats 1, 2, 3, 4; upstrokes on all the "ands," (1 *and* 2 *and* 3 *and* 4 *and).* It's not important whether you're playing whole, half, quarter, or eighth notes; rather, you need to consider where they fall in the measure. If you pick a note on beats 1, 2, 3, or 4, begin with a downstroke. If you pick a note on the "and" between any of the beats, begin with an upstroke. Keep this up-and-down pattern intact even when you switch strings. For example, if you are playing on string three and are going down in pitch to strings four, five, or six, your tendency might be to use an upstroke where a downstroke is expected. Resist the temptation! It'll only mess up your rhythm. Throughout the music you've seen suggested pick directions in those spots that might be confusing. A downstroke is noted with a ⌃ and an upstroke with a ⌄ .

The rule for both hands is to move them as little as possible. Use short, relaxed strokes with your picking hand; move the fingers of your fretting hand only as far off the fingerboard as necessary to play cleanly. Any extra motion is wasted.

I can't stress enough how important a relaxed approach is. Your natural tendency will be to tense up, to bear down, to *squeeze* those notes out, especially at tempos slightly beyond your reach. You may also find yourself tightening up to play louder in group situations. (The acoustic guitarist's nightmare is a jam session with about four loud banjo players. Try to get them to quiet down and listen when you play leads. Explain that if you can't hear yourself, they and the audience can't hear you either.)

In the long run the tension will put an upper limit on both your ability to play fast and your ability to play for extended periods of time. After playing guitar for over 20 years, I still find tension my main enemy. I have guitarist friends who have developed tendonitis or back problems due to this playing tension. Frank Wakefield, the great mandolinist, recommends a very loose and limber picking-hand wrist for both guitar and mandolin. He characterizes the motion as "letting your wrist shake your hand."

Think of guitar playing as an athletic endeavor and develop an approach to playing that won't hurt you. Warm up, just like a baseball pitcher, before you tear into a high-speed tune. Remember that the point of a warmup exercise, like those on the following pages, is to warm up. They're not meant to impress whoever is within earshot.

Playing at faster speeds is usually more difficult than playing at slower speeds. If you have trouble at a fast speed, slow it down a little and work your way up gradually. Chart your progress with a metronome. Set a goal, which may be to play **"Sally Johnson"** at metronome setting 96, and approach it first from, say, one half the target speed. Gradually work up to speed, watching for signs of tightness and tension.

Also realize that, just like an athlete, there will be a certain amount of soreness in your hand and arm muscles and fretting fingertips as they develop. This is quite normal and shouldn't hold you back. If it's *very* painful, you're probably doing something *very* wrong and you should seek the professional advice of a doctor and a good music teacher.

The height of the strings above your fingerboard, called **"action,"** is an important factor here, too. If the strings are too far above the fingerboard, you can fatigue both hands in minutes. If your action is too low, your tone and volume will suffer and some notes will tend to buzz. Try different guitars and decide what type of action fits the way you play. If you don't yet know what's best for you, choose something in the middle. You can always change it as you grow. As you experiment, you'll find your own happy medium. Here again, a good teacher can help you choose a guitar that's easy to play.

★    ★    ★    ★    ★    ★    ★    ★

The following exercises are designed to help you warm up while improving your up-and-down picking. Even up-and-down picking is essential to good lead flatpicking. Begin working with these exercises at a slow metronome setting. You'll probably tend to have a strong downstoke, since gravity is helping, and a weak and less controlled upstroke; so concentrate on evening them out. You may find that you have particular problems on the fourth, fifth, and sixth strings, especially if you anchor your pinkie or fist on the pickguard near string one. That can be quite a stretch. Work most on whatever gives you trouble. Why practice what comes easy?

The first exercise is based on a descending G arpeggio. You can play it, and most of these exercises, anywhere up and down the neck. Construct a complete exercise by moving it up fret by fret as far as you can go on the neck and then back down. Play along with a metronome to keep your time honest. Pay close attention to the pick-direction markings.

The next two exercises are chromatic; that is, they use every note of the chromatic scale, every adjacent note and fret on the fingerboard. The first of these is the G♯ chromatic scale and uses open strings. The second is the C chromatic scale in a closed, and thus moveable, position. You'll notice that the G and C chromatic scales, like every other chromatic scale, have identical notes. They just begin and end at different spots. Be sure to practice moving the C chromatic form everywhere on the neck and across the strings.

With the ascending/descending exercises, I suggest that you work with one region of the neck each time you practice, rather than trying to hit all the possibilities each session. For example, one day you could work on the first two strings, as shown, moving up and down the neck, descending on string one, ascending on string two. At your next practice session you might work this same pattern across all the strings from one to six and attempt to keep your hand position as constant as possible. A third variation could be to work any other pair of strings as you did in the first example. Remember that the B and G pair will not have exactly the same pattern as the others. If you're not sure why that is, check out the tablature to the G♯ and C chromatic scales.

The last two exercises use the A natural minor and C major scale forms. Again you'll notice that these two scales have identical notes. (The A natural minor has a special relationship to C major. It is called the relative minor of the C scale. Both the major key and its relative minor have the same notes and the same key signature — in the case of C and Am, no sharps or flats. The sixth tone of every major scale is the root of its relative minor scale — for example, Em for G, Dm for F. Chart 6 on page 17 will give you a handy reference for relative minors.) Each scale shown begins with a different left-hand finger and will help coordinate your right and left hands. Both are in closed positions and moveable. Make sure that you practice both in all keys. Don't forget to try the Am scale in triplets!

These exercises will also help you discover which fretting-hand finger to use with any given hand and fret position. Obviously you can fret any note with your index, second, third, or fourth fingers, or sometimes even your thumb. You get into trouble when you have to play the next note smoothly and easily without doing finger backflips. You'll find a few fingering suggestions in the music. Remember: The basic rule is to move your hands as little but as logically as possible. Check out Bill Bay's *Guitar Handbook* (Mel Bay MB94135) for a complete set of scales and exercises.

It's important to start making up your own exercises to drill your trouble spots and to give yourself interesting variations. I've listed the beginnings of some variations you can complete. Get in the habit of playing any exercise all over the neck. Remember that most notes on the guitar can be played on more than one string and in different positions. Experiment. Try to make up two or three variations for every scale or lick shown in this book. Keep in mind that speed is totally unimportant in these exercises. Work to coordinate and strengthen your fingers and to learn scales and picking technique.

# Exercise 23

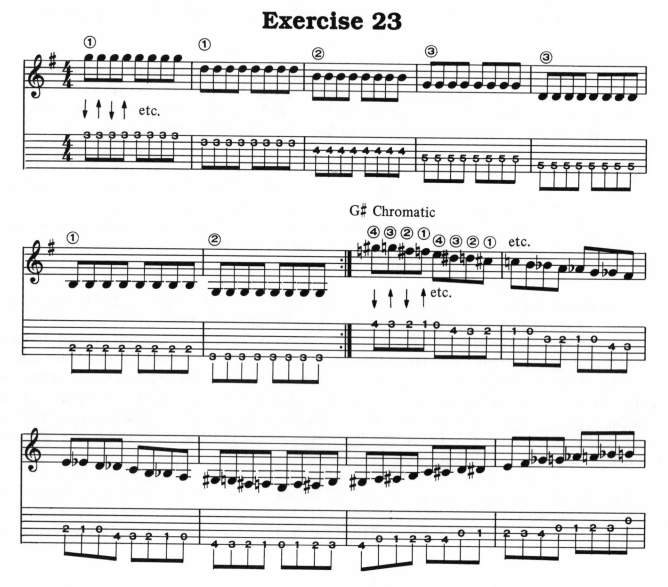

70

71

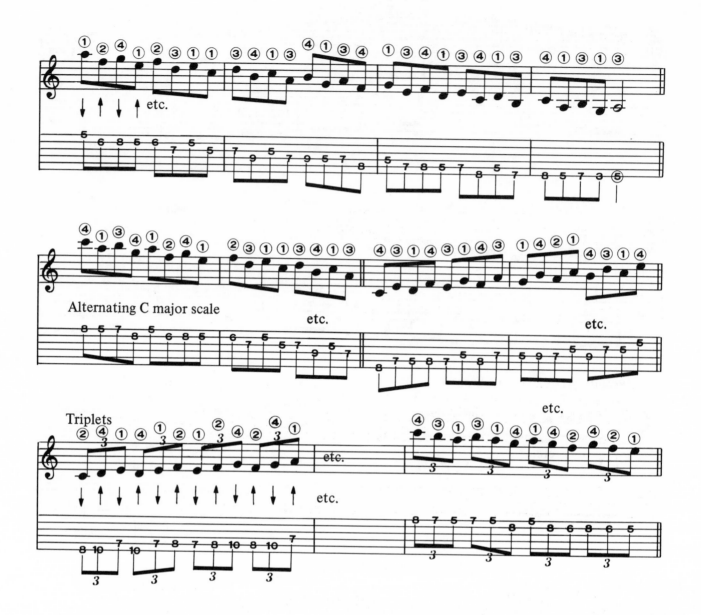

Alternating C major scale

Triplets

72

# "Sally Johnson"

Fiddle tunes account for the vast majority of the lead flatpicking repertoire. **"Sally Johnson"** is our first fiddle tune written in a straight lead style with mostly eighth notes and no chord strums punctuating melodic phrases. I heard this version of **"Sally Johnson"** at a guitar contest years ago. It's almost identical to another tune called **"Katy Hill."**

**"Sally Johnson"** is great for encouraging you to play in other neck positions. The first part is played "up the neck" in mostly closed **"fifth position."** Fifth position is so named because the first finger of your fretting hand plays its notes in the 5th fret. Your fretting hand should loiter in that general area. In measure 7 you'll switch to seventh position. In the second part you'll slip back down to what's basically second position with lots of open-string notes. Notice how both parts are built on the repetition, with slight changes, of their first measures. You'll find this to be true with most fiddle tunes. You end up having to memorize only about half of what's shown — the rest is repetition. Since the melodies are structured with repetition, don't be afraid to approach your soloing the same way.

★　　　★　　　★　　　★　　　★　　　★　　　★　　　★

Lead acoustic guitar is relatively new in bluegrass music. The Stanley Brothers were virtually the only first-generation band to incorporate lead guitar, as played by George Shuffler, into their original sound. Occasionally other bands would feature lead guitar as a novelty part of their acts. I'm sure it was due in part to the problem of making an acoustic guitar heard over the din of banjo, mandolin, bass, and fiddle.

In the '60s and '70s, players like Doc Watson, Clarence White, Tony Rice, Dan Crary, Don Reno, and Norman Blake popularized lead acoustic guitar and brought it up to the artistic level of the other lead bluegrass and folk instruments. Flatpicking contests became a standard part of most fiddle contests, and records of flatpicking began to be produced.

Some of the players, like Watson and Blake, have rarely played lead acoustic guitar on bluegrass standards in the context of a traditional bluegrass band. It's ironic that they've had such a major impact on flatpicking in bluegrass groups. Other players, like White, Rice, Crary, and Reno, were usually found in the bluegrass context swatting it out with the others in the struggle to be heard. These days, better microphones, electronics, and a dynamic sensitivity among supporting players make lead acoustic guitar more of a possibility than ever before.

Backup for fiddle tunes is virtually identical to the basic "bass-strum" backup you've already studied. Runs, connecting licks, hammers, pulls, slides, etc., should all be incorporated. The most important point, though, is to give the lead player a solid and inspiring background. Strive for good time and a good groove. Be supportive and don't compete with the lead player. Your immediate job is to make the lead player sound good. That will in turn make the group sound good. When it's your turn to solo, the others should support you in a like manner.

Great guitarists get to be great guitarists by challenging themselves and pushing their limits. When they learn a tune, a solo, or a lick, they use it as a basis for further exploration. They build on the known to learn the unknown. You need to do the same. Don't let yourself be satisfied with the set pieces that you learn, especially pieces from this book. I've included a few possibilities for expanding the version of **"Sally Johnson"** shown.

It's always good to know how to play a melody or chord progression in several places on the neck, in several keys. Make it a personal rule to learn every melody in at least two octaves and two different keys. Move the first part of **"Sally Johnson"** down an octave; move the second part up an octave. I've given you a few measures to get you started.

Since you already know the melody to the first part in a closed position, try moving it up 2 frets to the key of A, or down 2 frets to the key of F. If you keep your fretting-hand position intact from the key-of-G version and follow the G fingering guide (circled numbers above the staff), it'll be easy.

Next try mixing in some open strings with the closed-position notes in the original melody's seventh and eighth measures. You'll get a beautiful ringing effect. Once you've moved the original melody to the second part up an octave, try experimenting with different combinations of closed and open notes.

# Tune 24: "Sally Johnson"

# More Keys and Positions

The keys of G and C are very popular with guitarists because they offer so many open-string and easily fretted notes. They're also quite comfortable keys for bass notes and runs. We tend to learn tunes in either G or C, rather than F or B♭ (or, heaven forbid, something like E♭!), and then capo up to reach any other keys.

On the other hand, fiddlers and mandolinists favor A and D for the relatively easy reaches those keys offer on *their* respective instruments. Often the fiddler knows a tune in A or D and the guitarist knows it in G or C. If one doesn't know the other's key, no music gets played. In most cases the guitarist slaps the trusty capo onto the 2nd fret and plays in G or C. While this can be a happy compromise in the short run, it's very limiting to the guitarist in the long run.

I have nothing against those easy keys, positions, or capos, and I use them all the time. They offer certain sounds that you can't get any other way. The problem comes with limiting yourself to these keys. You'll miss out on the special sounds the other keys like open A, E, D, B♭, and F offer. You end up not using two thirds of your guitar. The next few tunes will encourage you to explore other positions and keys.

# Salt Creek

**"Salt Creek"** is usually played in the key of A. Guitarists play it in G capoed position at the 2nd fret. Here's your chance to turn the flatpicking world on its ear by learning **"Salt Creek"** in both capoed G and open A. You'll be the idol of millions! The process will give you practice in relating different keys on the guitar neck. Ultimately it will free you to play any melody in any key, closed or open position.

It is a bit more difficult to play **"Salt Creek"** in A without the capo, but give it a try. Both G and A versions are included here. They are slightly different to accommodate easier position playing. See if you can discover the differences and the reasons for them. In the A version, first part, first ending, you have a slide on the last note (F♯— fourth string, 4th fret) to take you back to the first note of the tune. Unfortunately the first note is on the third string, 2nd fret, making such a slide difficult. Instead slide on the fourth string from the 4th to the 7th fret. Play the first A note at the 7th fret of string four and then move to the A at the 2nd fret of string three.

The second endings are quite different from the first endings, although both have a bluesy feel. You can, with minor modification, interchange them. You can also lift both and use them elsewhere as runs. First endings in both keys have string stretches where you push the string of the note in parentheses to slightly raise its pitch. Notice the position change from first to fifth in measure 5 of Part One. The whole second part is quite a stretch.

Once you've memorized **"Salt Creek"** as written in G, work on the A version. Then try replacing all the open-string notes in the A version with closed-position notes. This will give you a moveable melody that you can play in closed B♭ or A♭.

Try substituting a half-note F for the half-note G in the fourth measure of the second part. Which do you prefer? Experiment with the same spot in the key-of-A version. I've always played the G half note over the F chord and have only recently noticed that the substituted F note would make for a better note/chord match. Ah, the wisdom of advanced age!

# Tune 25a: "Salt Creek" in G

# Tune 25b: "Salt Creek" in A

# "Bury Me Beneath the Willow"

**"Bury Me Beneath the Willow"** is another great old Carter Family song. Like **"Sally Johnson,"** it'll give you practice in playing in two positions an octave apart.

If you're used to playing in G and C, you may find that some of these notes are a stretch to reach. The more you practice, the easier it will be. Don't forget the modified "barre" A you used in **"Corinna."** Spend some extra time on the transitions between Carter style and the straight eighth-note picking in measures 14 and 30–31. In the second, higher-octave version, you'll see a few "arpeggiated" strums where you let the individual notes ring out. The last note to sound should be your melody note.

Play **"Bury Me Beneath the Willow"** with another guitarist. Have him or her capo at the 5th fret. Which chords should they use? Review Chart 6 on page 17. Write them in pencil over the chords you play.

**Lyrics:**

My heart is sad and I am lonely
For the only one I love
When shall I see her, oh no never
'Til we meet in heaven above.

Chorus: Bury me beneath the willow
Under the weeping willow tree
When she hears that I am sleeping
Then perhaps she'll think of me.

She told me that she dearly loved
How could I believe it untrue
Until the angels softly whispered
"She will prove untrue to you."

Tomorrow was to be our wedding
God, oh God, where can she be
She's out a'courting with another
And no longer cares for me.

# Tune 26: "Bury Me Beneath the Willow"

melody 1

melody 2

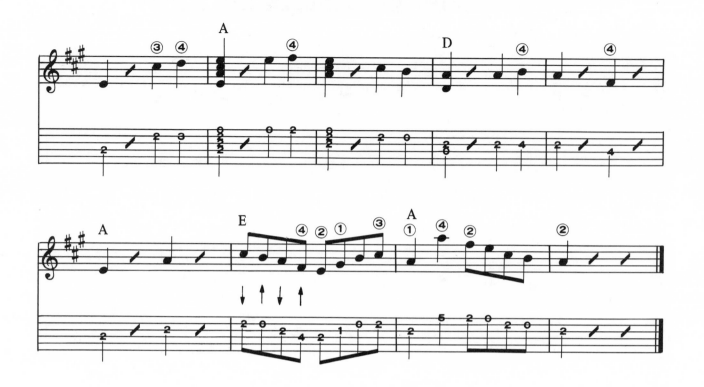

# "Arkansas Traveller"

**"Arkansas Traveller"** is a fiddle classic, another "must know" tune. Most fiddlers perform it in the key of D. On the following pages, you'll find the melody and a number of exercises with positions, keys, and octaves.

The basic melody is in second position. All the notes are fretted, none on open strings, until you get to the seventh and eighth measures. Once you've learned the melody as written with open strings, change these two measures to closed-position notes. This melodic passage is repeated at the end of the second part. Once you can do this, you have the entire melody in a closed, and thus moveable, position.

Slide the whole thing up 2 frets to the key of E, just like you did with **"Sally Johnson."** Maintain the exact fretting-hand position as you slide up and down the neck transposing. You'll use the same fingerings as noted in the circled numbers above the staff. The first two measures of each part are included here. Complete the rest in your notebook. Now move the whole tune up another 3 frets to the key of G, then 1 more fret to A♭. Amazing, huh? You can now play **"Arkansas Traveller"** in any key up and down the neck from the key of D♭ in first position to the key of C in the twelfth position.

For a great workout, start playing the tune slowly in the key of D♭. On the repeat of the first part, move up to D. At the second part, move up to E♭. On the repeat of the second part, move up to E natural. Keep going through the tune until you're as far up the neck as you can go. Then start back down. Oh, the joys of closed-position playing! It's just like having your own built-in capo. So far you're doing great, but stay tuned — you're not off the hook yet.

Let's backtrack and figure out **"Arkansas Traveller"** in D, an octave lower than the original version, using open-string notes. We'll have to modify measures 6 and 7 of the first part since our melody needs two notes, C♯ and D, that are lower than the open sixth-string E. Once you learn this version, try other keys in this same position by starting first on the open third or G string and then on the open fifth or A string. In the A version, you'll need to change the sixth and seventh measures as above with the D. I have included a few measures to get you started.

Another variation you can try in the open-D version is to lower your sixth-string E one whole step to a D note. This allows you to end on the low-note D with your ending licks like 6 and 7. It makes for quite an interesting sound.

# Tune 27a: "Arkansas Traveller"

# Tune 27b: Exercises

# "Billy in the Lowground"

This version of the fiddle tune **"Billy in the Lowground"** demonstrates position switching from basic open first to closed fifth, indicated in the tablature. The fifth-position version is modified slightly in a couple of spots to save your fretting hand from having to move too much.

Learn the "open," bottom-of-the-neck melody first. If you're not used to playing up the neck, this version will be quite a bit easier than the other. Notice that the last two C notes in the eighth measure of Part One are connected. The symbol between the notes is called a **"tie"** and looks like a slur. The only difference is that a tie connects two notes of the same pitch; a slur, two notes of different pitches. When playing two tied notes, we pick only the first and let it ring over the time value of the second. (Remember that, when we count measures, No. 1 begins after the two-eighth-note introduction.)

Once you know the melody down the neck, learn the closed-position version. I know, I know, it's difficult. Still, it's the only way to make the transition to closed-position playing. You just have to sweat it for a while. The fingering suggestions (circled numbers in the tab) should help you. Remember that closed-position playing will ultimately free you to play any song in any key. It's for your own good, kids! It'll help you grow up to be a complete guitar player.

Measure 4 of the first part of the closed-position melody is difficult to play smoothly unless you use a technique called **"finger-rolling"** to move from the fourth-string G note, 5th fret, to the fifth-string D note, also 5th fret. Use your second finger and, rather than picking it up and off the fourth string, 5th fret, to move it to string five, simply roll it over.

Once you've learned the closed version, move it around until you get the feel of other keys. Use it as warmup exercise. Finally, try the hammer-pull variations for Part One, measure 4.

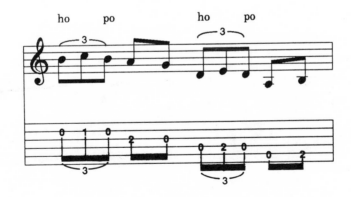

# Tune 28a: "Billy in the Lowground" (Open Position)

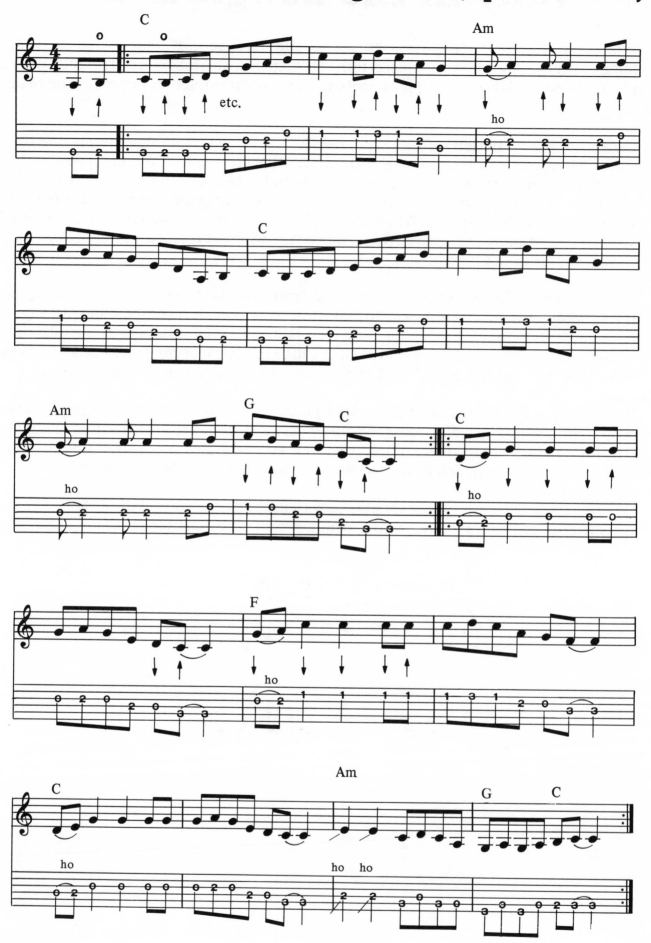

# Tune 28b: "Billy in the Lowground" (Closed Position)

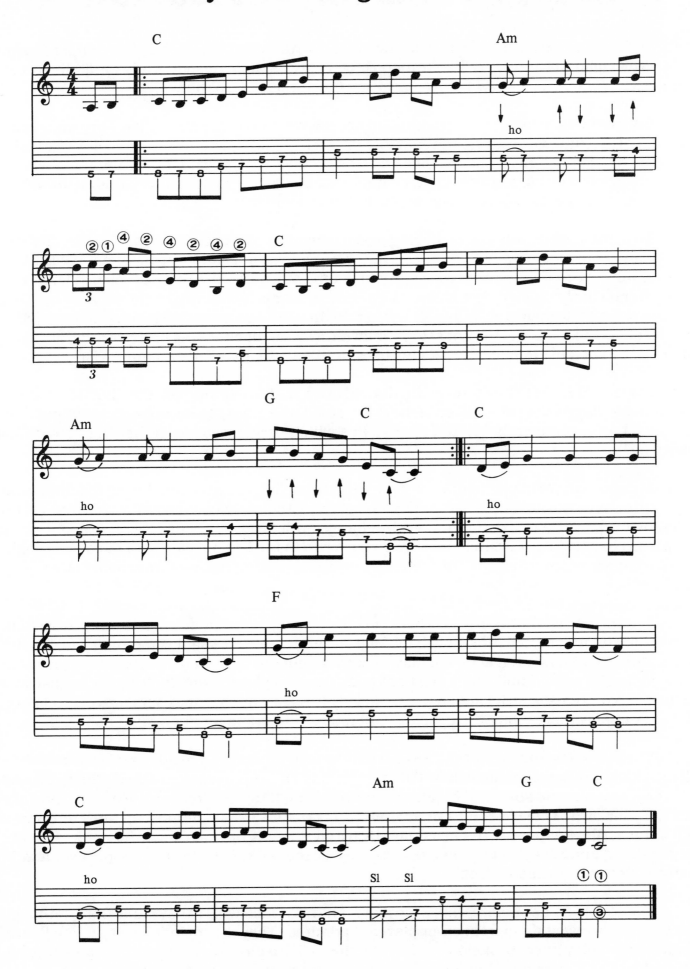

# Soloing and Improvisation

So far we've looked at chords, bass notes and strums, bass runs, basic accompaniment, Carter-style lead playing, lead fills, transposing, capos, simple melody leads on fiddle tunes, and position playing. Now we'll move on to soloing and improvisation.

**Improvising** is much like speaking. In speech we train ourselves by learning words and sentence structure and study how to combine these elements to communicate feelings verbally. In music we learn notes, chords, licks, phrases, and the process of combining them to communicate our feelings musically. True improvisation is the process of creating as the music flows, not reading from sheet music or playing from memory.

To many people, this is a confusing and frightening concept. *"How could I ever do that? How will I know what to play?"* In my view, it's as easy as speaking. At the most basic level, musical improvisation is like telling a story in your own words. At a more developed level, you might significantly change that story. At its most advanced, you might invent new musical phrases or drop the known story line altogether. Right now you can improvise on that most basic level by simply playing any tune or solo your own way without changing much of anything. You don't have to be able to make up 16 choruses on the fly to qualify as an improvisor.

Players are often hung up with that idea of making it up "on the fly." Most great improvisors play in the personal style they've created and often repeat themselves. What they have is a bag of phrases, licks, and approaches which they *assemble*, rather than *create*, as they play.

My approach to improvising is to begin with the melody. Learn it inside and out, in several keys, in several positions. In the process of playing the melody over and over, along with listening to other players perform it, slight changes will begin to occur to you. It might be as simple as changing an introduction or inverting a run in the last measure of a melody. It might be as complex as inverting the entire melody or incorporating phrases from some other song or player.

I strive to keep the melody on which I'm improvising in the forefront of the improvisation. I often fail and find myself musically babbling! Jethro Burns once said something like, "I want the audience to know what song I'm playing if they come back from the restroom when I'm in the middle of a solo." I find that I most enjoy listening to players who include me in that way in their explorations. A strict adherence to melody is not really the main point; rather, it is that one should play "something the peoples understand," to quote an anonymous blues singer.

These last few tunes, for the most part fiddle tunes, present a melody and improvisation along with short descriptions of how I'm approaching the improvisation. Check them out and use them as a place to start, but be sure to add your own touches. You don't want to sound like me! On your own, **1) learn the basic melody, 2) transpose that melody up and/or down a full octave, 3) transpose it to closed position and move it up and down the neck, 4) begin improvising simply by changing a few melody notes, licks, or inverting a phrase, and 5) write it down in your notebook.**

I've played some of these things for years. I have no idea where they came from, although I suspect I borrowed them from other players I admired. They are included so that you'll have something to play after the melody. Hopefully they will inspire you to concoct your own solos. The *Advanced Flatpicking Handbook* will cover improvisation in greater detail.

# "Sally Goodin"

Every fiddler plays **"Sally Goodin."** Learn the easy melody first, then the variations, and yes, you can use your capo at the 2nd fret (whew, finally!). Notice how the first part of the melody is in second position (first finger plays in the 2nd fret), and the second part of the melody is in first position (first finger plays in the 1st fret). Try playing the entire part in one or the other position.

Solo No. 1 is a slight variation on the melody. The pickup notes at the very beginning are changed, as are the last two measures of each part. All I did was graft different end licks onto the melodic phrases. These substitutions can be used in hundreds of other tunes. I suggest that you start a section in your notebook for generic phrases like these. Use the same basic fretting-hand positions you used on the melody. Once you've got that down, try first position on Part One, second position on Part Two. Is one position easier than the other? Which fingers seem weak or uncoordinated? Practice the position that's most difficult and exercise the finger that's weak.

Solo No. 2 takes you up the neck to seventh position. Solo No. 3 goes back down to second. This last solo presents a technique that you may not be familiar with: **double stops.** Instead of playing just one note at a time, you play two in harmony.

Challenge yourself by combining and recombining all these different licks, phrases, and parts into new solos. Although these solos are written with repeats, I rarely play a repeated part exactly as I did it the first time through. Change them slightly on the repeats. Build your vocabulary while practicing your ability to make up solos from parts. For extra practice, move the positions for the original open-G version to the fifth and fourth strings for A and D versions respectively, just like you did with **"Late Last Night"** and **"Arkansas Traveller."**

## Tune 29: "Sally Goodin"

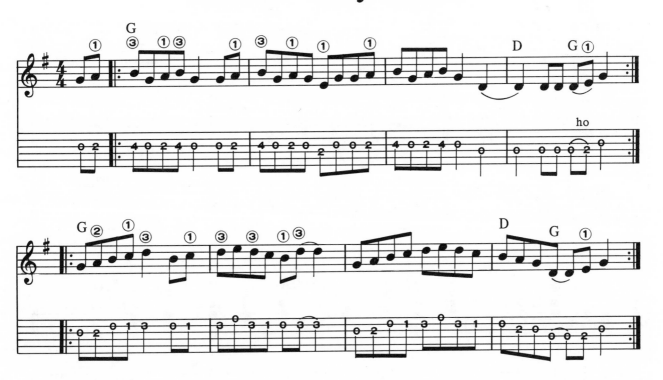

# "Beaumont Rag"

I love playing **"Beaumont Rag."** It has a great swingy lilt together with a good country groove. It's one of those mammoth tunes that loom large in the legend of old-time and blue-grass music.

For years I played it in open C position capoed up 2 frets to be in D. After tons of flack from fiddlers who played it in the key of F, I finally learned this version in F without a capo. Now I'm covered either way! Notice how the same melodic fragments are repeated again and again.

The first part of **"Beaumont Rag"** is in a closed position, so you can move it back down to D if you need to. The second part, with its open-string cross picking, will take a little adjusting to transpose; but it shouldn't be too difficult. Check the pick-direction markings and notice that they change direction after every note. My basic pattern is:

**"down-up-down, up-down-up, etc."**
**4      3      2      4      3      2**

and I don't deviate from it. When I play this part, I hold a partial C chord (see the diagram) and use the fourth finger of my fretting hand to play the D notes (second string, 3rd fret) that occur in both the C and F patterns.

The first part of the solo is a restatement of the melody without too much improvisatory interference. The second is similar in approach but a bit farther removed from the stated melody. It's a pattern that ascends and descends to complete the part. The first lick of the second part looks like this:

Try playing it in a different position starting on the fifth string, 6th fret, E♭ note. Start with your third finger. *Hint:* Play the following C note on the third string, 5th fret, first finger. Since this lick and its cousin an octave higher are closed-position licks, they'll be useful on other chords in other keys.

When playing the solo, use the positions and fingerings suggested in the melody. You should also experiment with a few other positions to see what works best for you. There's no set rule other than the logic of moving your hands as little as possible, so ultimately you'll have to decide how best to play any given passage.

# Tune 30a: "Beaumont Rag" Melody

# Tune 30b: "Beaumont Rag" Solo

# "Temperance Reel"

Most of **"Temperance Reel"** is straightforward flatpicking. The pickup triplet is played with one pick stroke on the open D string followed by two hammers on the 2nd and 4th frets. You can also play it with three separate pick strokes, but it won't sound as smooth as with the hammers.

The first solo is really another version of the melody that I heard somewhere. I often play it as my repeat of the first-part melody. You'll notice it has a hammer-pull combination move similar to the fourth-measure variation on **"Billy in the Lowground."** The second part is really just an extended lick that I use quite often when I come across an Em chord.

In the second solo you'll see the notation **"8va,"** which means to play the notes an octave higher than they are written in the standard notation. If you're reading tab, ignore this direction. Some phrases in this solo leave the melody behind. It comes dangerously close to hokum by breaking my "keep-the-melody-in-the-forefront" rule. That's OK here, though, since the melody has been very well stated by the time this solo is heard. If you perform it in a similar context, it'll be fine. If, however, everything that has come before and after you is non-melodic, you might want to sneak more of the melody into your solo.

## Tune 31a: "Temperance Reel" Melody

# Tune 31b: "Temperance Reel" Solos

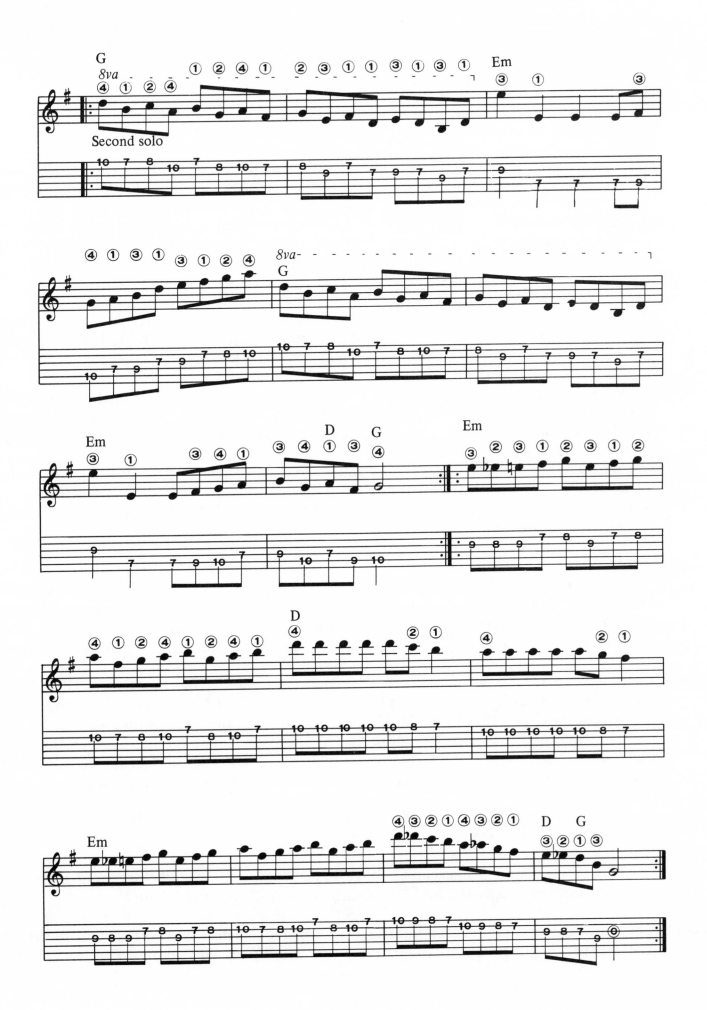

**Congratulations!** You've completed this book and now have a working knowledge of flatpicking! Keep playing, listening, and learning. Check into the sources on the next few pages. Write me c/o Musix, P.O. Box 231005, Pleasant Hill, CA 94523 with your comments and jokes. See you soon with the *Advanced Flatpicking Handbook!*

# Discography

In general you should look for bluegrass and guitar records that *you* like. Throughout this book I've mentioned players *I* like very much who have influenced me. Here's a brief compilation:

**Original Carter Family:** Almost any recording illustrates Carter-style backup and lead. Make sure the recordings are from the late 1920s or 1930s. *Twenty of the Best* (RCA Germany 89369) and *The Best of...* (Columbia 9189).

**Doc & Merle Watson:** You can't go wrong with any of Doc's records. I especially like *Doc Watson on Stage* (Vanguard VSD 9/10), *The Essential* (VMS 73108 and 73121), *Doc Watson & Son* (Vanguard VRS-9170), and *Doc & Merle Watson's Guitar Album* (Flying Fish 301). My favorite is *Lester Flatt & Earl Scruggs with Doc Watson* (Columbia CS 9443).

**The Stanley Brothers:** A major component of the Stanley sound is the excellent lead guitar work of George Shuffler. You'll find lots of lead on *16 Greatest Gospel Hits* (Gusto GT-0016), *16 Greatest Hits* (Gusto SD-3003), and *20 Bluegrass Originals* (Gusto GD-5026X).

**Clarence White:** Anything with the original Kentucky Colonels will blow your sox off. *Appalachian Swing* (Liberty LN 10185) is excellent! Also check out *The White Brothers* (Rounder 0073), *Clarence White and the Kentucky Colonels* (Rounder 0098), and *The Kentucky Colonels On Stage* (Rounder 0199).

**Bill Monroe:** You'll especially like the all instrumental records like *Master of Bluegrass* (MCA 5214), *Bill Monroe's Uncle Pen* (MCA 500), and *Bluegrass Instrumentals* (MCA 104); but don't expect any lead guitar work. You'll have to learn from fiddle and mandolin. *Feast Here Tonight* (RCA Bluebird AXM2-5510) by the Monroe Brothers has a great collection of songs, and Charlie Monroe's backup playing is a wonderful source of runs and ideas.

**Tony Rice:** They're all wonderful. I especially recommend *Skaggs and Rice* (Sugar Hill 3711), *Rice & Blake* (Rounder 0233), any of the five volumes of *The Bluegrass Album* (Rounder), or *Tony Rice—Guitar* (King KB 529). You'll find more modern tunes and sounds on his work in the David Grisman Quintet on the album of the same name (Kaleidoscope F-5) *(don't miss this!)* or any of his Tony Rice Unit albums on Rounder. *The Bluegrass Albums* don't have a great deal of lead flatpicking on them, but they're great anyway.

**Norman Blake:** Above with Rice, *The Rising Fawn String Ensemble* (Rounder 0122), and *Full Moon on the Farm* (Rounder 0144).

**Dan Crary**: *Bluegrass Guitar* (American Heritage 401.27) *(A must! Probably the first LP to feature lead flatpicking throughout.)* and *Dan Crary—Guitar* (Sugar Hill 3730).

**Dix Bruce**: I'm on a couple cuts of each of these recordings: *End of the Rainbow*—Frank Wakefield (Bay 214) and *Blues Stay Away From Me* — Frank Wakefield (Takoma 7082).

I've just released two new casette tapes, *My Folk Heart* (Musix C-101), a collection of American folk and old-time songs, on which I flatpick and fingerpick the guitar, play a little mandolin and sing my folk heart out, and *Tuxedo Blues* (C-102), a band recording with me on guitar and vocals, Bob Alekno on mandolin, Dave Balakrishnan on violin and Mike Wollenberg on bass, of mostly originals in the New Acoustic Music mode. We just don't take it quite as seriously as them Windham Hill fellers. Both tapes are available from Musix, P.O. Box 231005, Pleasant Hill, CA 94523.

Some of these recordings may be difficult to find. The best mail-order source I know is Downhome Records, 10341 San Pablo Avenue, El Cerrito, CA 94530. These folks specialize in hard-to-get folk, bluegrass, and acoustic string music. When you write to request prices, enclose an SASE.

# Bibliography

In general, look for books that have anything to do with flatpicking, guitar, country and folk, bluegrass or fiddle tunes. There are probably hundreds of different folk song collections available. Choose one with at least some familiar tunes and make it a point to learn the others.

Some of the books listed below are tough to find. The 5th String, 3051 Adeline Street, Berkeley, CA 94703 stocks most and sells mail order. You can also write to me c/o Musix, P.O. Box 231005, Pleasant Hill, CA 94523, and I'll pass on whatever availability information I have. When you write to either address, enclose an SASE.

*Bill Monroe: 200 Bluegrass Specials* (Hansen House 82-58): Nice collection of songs from the folk and bluegrass repertoire along with a few Monroe original tunes.

*The Folksinger's Word Book* by Fred and Irwin Silber (Oak 000140): Over *one thousand* sets of lyrics with chords noted. No standard notation or tab. If you like to sing, this book should be in your collection.

*Slim Richey's Bluegrass Word Book, Vol. 1 & 2* (Ridge Runner): Another great lyric collection. No music, and not all entries have chord changes written in.

*Fiddle Tunes & Irish Music for Guitar* by Dan Gelo (Mel Bay MB94020): Fine source of Celtic tunes.

*The Fiddler's Fakebook, Guitar Edition* by David Brody (Oak): Amazing compilation of the most popular tunes of the genre referenced to recordings so you can hear them first hand (or ear). My big beef with this book is that it has only tablature. You might learn more from buying the fiddle edition.

*Note-reading and Music Theory for Folk Guitarists* by Jerry Silverman (Oak): Nice introduction to theory.

*Music Fundamentals* by Elvo D'Amante (Encore Music Publishing, Orinda, CA): I took some of his classes at Laney College in Oakland, CA. He is, hands down, the best teacher I ever had.

# Notes

[1] **Short Music Theory Note:** Don't get confused with all the different numbers flying around. Previously we discussed beat numbers in measures. These numbers refer to notes in scales and chords. A chord is three or more notes strummed simultaneously. Chords are derived from the various major scales (do-re-me-fa-sol-la-ti-do).

The C major scale is:

| C | D | E | F | G | A | B | C |
|---|---|---|---|---|---|---|---|
| 1 | 2 | 3 | 4 | 5 | 6 | 7 | 8 |

The C major chord is made up of the 1, 3, and 5 of the scale or the notes C E G. (Remember that the "1" can also be called the "root.") When you play a C chord on the guitar you are sounding these notes, in some cases more than one of each note. (See Chart 3.) The C minor chord consists of 1 ♭3 5 of the C scale or C E♭G. ("♭" means to lower or "flat" the given note by one half step.) C7 is made up of 1 3 5 ♭7 or C E G B♭, and Cm7 is 1 ♭3 5 ♭7 or C E♭G B♭. Every major or minor chord follows these basic recipes. You can figure them out if you know the scales.

[2] Since Chart 6 tells you the major scales to all the keys, it can also help you transpose melodies note by note. For example, the first few notes of the melody of **"Worried Man Blues"** are Ds, E, G, and A. Since we're in the key of G transposing to the key of D in the example, we first find those notes on the horizontal G-key line, (ignoring the "m" and "o" chord designations), then follow each up one space to the key-of-D line, and make our substitutions. The D note becomes A, E becomes B, G becomes D, and A becomes E. If this seems a bit difficult right now, hold on. We'll work more with melody transposition later.

[3] Diminished-seven chords are rare in bluegrass and country music, but they do occur occasionally. I have good news and bad news. The bad news is that they aren't the easiest chords to fret; the good news is that one form or fingering is moveable along the neck and will provide all 12 (C, C♯/D♭, D, D♯/E♭, E, F, F♯/G♭, G, G♯/A♭, A, A♯/B♭, B) diminished chords. Wait, there's more good news! Any note in a diminished chord can name it. For example, the C diminished-seven chord has the notes C, E♭, G♭, A, so it can also be used as an E♭o, G♭o, or Ao. Likewise C♯o has the notes C♯, E, G, B♭ and can be used as Eo, Go, or B♭o. Finally, Do has the notes D, F, A♭, B and can be used as Fo, A♭o, or Bo. There are only three different diminished chords, so that gives you a one-in-three chance of hitting the right one! Don't confuse the diminished-seven chord (o or 07) with the half diminished chord (ø), which is also called a "minor-seven flat-five chord." The half diminished chord has an entirely different sound and function than the diminished seven.